From computerized "back offices" in New York banks to semiconductor production lines in Silicon Valley, the American workplace is being transformed. Dazzling new computer capabilities not only are redrawing the contours of working life, but are inspiring a revolution in social attitudes and cultural expectations, one that elevates the corporation—call it the "brave new workplace"—to a central eminence in American life.

In this utopian work world, the discontents and social conflicts that have plagued working life for centuries melt away. The new computer technology becomes the harbinger of satisfying, meaningful work; the corporation, no longer an impersonal bureaucracy, is a caring community; and business enterprise becomes the basic source of personal and social identity.

But is this in fact the case? Are not new inequities and social conflicts infecting America's corporate utopias? Part investigative journalism, part oral history, part political and cultural analysis, *Brave New Workplace* takes a searching look at the real world behind the alluring and dangerous new image of corporate happiness. Robert Howard demonstrates how corporations are using new technologies to expand managerial control at the expense of worker satisfaction, autonomy, and even efficiency. He examines the working lives of technology managers, management consultants, telephone operators, data-entry workers, and other technicians who serve the brave new workplace, bear its costs, and struggle to make it reflect their goals.

Lastly, Mr. Howard suggests ways for us to win social and political control over the workplace, arguing that we must keep it open to all Americans, not merely to a corporate, technological elite.

BRAVE NEW WORKPLACE

BRAVE
NEW
WORKPLACE

ROBERT HOWARD

88-106

ELISABETH SIFTON BOOKS

VIKING

ELISABETH SIFTON BOOKS • VIKING
Viking Penguin Inc., 40 West 23rd Street,
New York, New York 10010, U.S.A.
Penguin Books Ltd, Harmondsworth, Middlesex, England
Penguin Books Australia Ltd, Ringwood, Victoria, Australia
Penguin Books Canada Limited, 2801 John Street,
Markham, Ontario, Canada L3R 1B4
Penguin Books (N.Z.) Ltd, 182–190 Wairau Road,
Auckland 10, New Zealand

First published in 1985 by Viking Penguin Inc.
Published simultaneously in Canada

LIBRARY OF CONGRESS CATALOGING IN PUBLICATION DATA
Howard, Robert, 1954–
  Brave new workplace.
  "Elisabeth Sifton books."
  Includes index.
  1. Quality of work life—United States.   2. Corporate culture—United
States.   3. Labor supply—United States—Effect of technological innovations
on.   4. Work.   I. Title.
HD6957.U6H69   1985   306'.36   83-40639
ISBN 0-670-18738-0

Printed in the United States of America by
R. R. Donnelley & Sons Company, Harrisonburg, Virginia
Set in Times Roman

For My Parents

EDITORIAL NOTE

THIS IS A BOOK ABOUT CHANGE, and many of the people who appear in these pages have since moved on to other jobs. I have decided to retain the original institutional affiliations, even though some are now out of date. Needless to say, the comments of all represent personal opinions and not necessarily the official policies of the institutions where they work. In a few cases, I have chosen to use pseudonyms or no names at all to protect the identity of my informants.

ACKNOWLEDGMENTS

MANY OF THE IDEAS IN THIS BOOK were first developed in the pages of *Working Papers* magazine. I should like to thank the staff of *Working Papers,* in particular former editor Bob Kuttner, for their consistent support.

The research was funded, in large part, by a grant from the Ford Foundation. As probably the last beneficiary of his presence at the foundation, I should especially like to thank Robert Schrank, who for ten years provided crucial financial assistance to researchers and writers studying the American workplace.

The award of a Copeland Fellowship allowed me to begin writing during a five-month stay at Amherst College in 1983. My thanks to Barry O'Connell for alerting me to this innovative program, which brings independent writers, artists, and scholars to the Amherst campus.

A great many people have helped me formulate the arguments in these pages, although some of them may not know it and, of course, none is responsible for the final form these arguments have taken. My special thanks to Paul Adler, Andy Banks, Judy Gregory, Lewis Hyde, George Kateb, Leo Marx, Kristin Nygaard, Bill Ravanesi, Annalee Saxenian, Lenny Siegel, and Patricia Vigderman.

Finally, there are three people whose advice and encouragement have literally made this book possible. Suzanne Gordon has been a faithful reader and critic from the very beginning. My editor Elisabeth Sifton has been all that a writer could ask for—enthusiastic, generous, and understanding. And Leslie Schneider has been both colleague and companion on a long and occasionally arduous journey. As she well knows, many of the insights in these pages are hers.

CONTENTS

BRAVE NEW WORKPLACE

INTRODUCTION

WORK, TECHNOLOGY, AND UTOPIA

FEW AREAS OF OUR LIVES evoke more profound ambivalence than the activity that goes by the name of work. On the one hand, work seems synonymous with promise. It is the means by which we nourish a sense of mastery and achievement in the world. It is the major activity through which we shape our ambitions and our talents and, thus, come to know ourselves. Work also takes us beyond the self. It is our link to society, our chief (and, for many, only) collective activity. Through our work, we dedicate ourselves to an end—a product or service, a professional or occupational group, a human community. In its inherently double nature—simultaneously personal and social—work quite simply makes us who we are.

And yet, how often do we think of work as little more than a burden and a problem. It is a source of persistent dissatisfaction, a realm hedged in by necessity and constraint, time irretrievably lost to that unavoidable task of "making" a living. In the apt words of one social researcher, work is "society's most heavily obligated sphere of life." And if the idea of work contains a promise, then the obligations of working life, for many, signify a promise rarely kept.

During the past decade, our ambivalence about work has been exacerbated by enormous and nearly permanent change. Social and demographic changes have redrawn the visage of the U.S. labor force, introducing new groups into the workplace—women, minorities, and the baby-boom generation of the young. Economic changes continue to spawn previously unheard-of industries and dispatch familiar ones into decline; to transform entire geographic regions, allocating some to boom and others to dislocation and decay; even to challenge the heretofore dominant position of American industry in the world economy. Most recently (and perhaps most visibly), rapid technological change is revolutionizing the very tools with which we do our work, putting into question traditional occupations, skills, and ideas about what work is.

All these changes have contributed to a widespread uncertainty about work. Are the high unemployment levels of recent years to become a permanent fixture of American working life? Can the economy provide the same kind of generalized prosperity that it produced in the 1950s and 1960s in the decades to come? Who will be the winners and who the losers in the new economy that appears to be growing up right before our eyes?

At the same time as these changes have engendered myriad questions about work, they have also inspired a new set of promises on the part of that social institution which, more than any other, has shaped the contours of our working life during the past century: the modern corporation. Precisely when work has become so unstable and unsure, American business has begun to articulate a remarkably ambitious vision for the social transformation of working life, a scenario for a future in which we can put aside our ambivalence about work once and for all.

This is a book about that vision. It is the story of what I call the "brave new workplace." The pages that follow describe the elements of that vision and the meanings they communicate and tell how it is being put into practice at workplaces across the country and throughout the economy. They also suggest why this emerging corporate blueprint for the future of work constitutes a danger—not only for workers but for American society as a whole.

Just what is this vision of the brave new workplace? Its signs are all around us. They can be found in the media, in the speeches of corporate executives, in best-selling books, sometimes even in the very architecture of working life. They all speak to us of a desired future, often using images deeply rooted in our past.

Consider, by way of introduction, a recent advertisement appearing in magazines and newspapers across the country. It features a familiar personality from America's past and a product that will be a fixture of America's future—the IBM Personal Computer. A Chaplinesque figure sits before the soft, off-white keyboard and ice-green screen, his face consumed with wonder and delight. Plucked from his imprisoning assembly line, stripped of his overalls and dressed in a pinstripe suit (so suddenly that his work boots remain, old and worn, a fitting contrast to the high-tech polish of the computer), the character made famous by Chaplin in *Modern Times* is plopped down in the middle of the twenty-first century.

"How to test drive the IBM Personal Computer," the headline reads, only the first in a long line of references to that twentieth-century archetype of freedom and mobility, the automobile. Liberated from the drudgery of his factory job, his chair tipped back, his hat blown clean away by a passing breeze, our former assembly-line worker is off on a wild, exhilarating ride into the future of work. As if to underline this message, the punchline of the ad informs us that the IBM Personal Computer is "a tool for modern times."

Designed to sell computers, this ad sells a promise as well. Charlie Chaplin was the first popular media figure to express the reality of alienating work on the assembly line. For more than a generation, his film *Modern Times* has provided the images governing how we see industrial work. And yet, here, Chaplin's factory worker finds fulfillment (and, from the look of his suit, a considerable raise in pay) through the wonders of new technology. The computer delivers him from the prison of dirty, boring, alienating work. Within the frame of the ad, the former critic of work becomes a persuasive advocate for technology and for the corporation itself. Through technology and the corporation that provides it, Chaplin seems to be telling us, we too can be, like him, test-driving the IBM Personal Computer. And our work can become a realm of freedom—fluid, infinitely mobile, freighted with enormous possibility.

This idea that new technology will usher in an era of more satisfying and meaningful work is a key element in the vision of the brave new workplace. What is interesting about this ad and its use of Chaplin is that it speaks to our fears about technology gone out of control, our becoming a mere appendage of the machine (remember Chaplin trapped in the maw of that voracious conveyor belt), and in doing so allays them.

A further elaboration on this theme comes from the ongoing celebration of "high technology" in American culture. It's not merely the fact that we are fascinated with the technology of the silicon chip and awed by the rapid economic growth of the industries that produce and work with it. High technology also seems to offer us something more, an alternative image of the corporation itself.

One after another, journalists have made pilgrimage to California's Silicon Valley. The reports they have sent back suggest that these corporations of the future, far from being impersonal technocratic bureaucracies, are in fact the embodiment of an egalitarian community. "It does not take long," James Fallows has written in the *Atlantic,* "for a visitor . . . to the area to sense an atmosphere different from that of the 'mature' manufacturing industries." Silicon Valley firms are "more flexible," says Fallows, and "less concerned with the normal trappings of rank." This "egalitarian and flexible structure," adds *New York Times* correspondent Steve Lohr, allows high-tech companies to "avoid the bureaucratic hierarchy characteristic of most firms."

The most committed champions of this theme have been the founders of Silicon Valley's successful high-tech corporations. Sounding less like corporate executives than social visionaries, they have elevated the idea of the entrepreneur to the status of a new social ethic. "The rest of the country, and even the rest of the world, doesn't have a very good idea about Silicon Valley," Steve Jobs, the almost legendary cofounder of Apple Computer, told an audience at the first Stanford Conference on Entrepreneurship in April 1982. "There is something going on here on a scale which has never been seen on the face of the earth." Jobs called it a "critical mass of entrepreneurial risk culture" and he claimed that it was producing an epochal social change. "A lot of people ask if Silicon Valley is ever going to be unionized," Jobs continued. "I say everybody's unionized. . . . There's much greater union here than I've seen anywhere. What we're starting to see is the redefinition of the corporation in America."

Thus, the brave new workplace concerns not only technology but community, the transformation of bureaucracy, the redefinition of the corporation. And once the new technology resolves the age-old problem of alienation and the corporation becomes an expression of unity and communal bonds, then the workplace itself will be a temple dedicated to the cultivation of the self.

From the moment you step off the elevator that ferries people to the Tenneco Employee Center built on top of a parking garage in downtown Houston, you have the feeling of entering a spacious cathedral. Perhaps it is the light streaming through the three-story-tall windows. Perhaps it is the silence broken only by the gentle gurgling of fountains, the muted sound of voices, a distant laugh. Whatever the reason, you are enveloped in a reverential atmosphere radiating tranquillity and calm.

A few steps from the elevator, you enter a lavish indoor tropical garden. Its bewildering variety of broadleaf plants and green bamboo shoots arch toward the sun. The employee cafeteria is right off the garden. It has green marble floors and tables, and chairs of powder-blue crushed velvet and bronze.

One floor down from the main entrance is the sanctuary of this modern-day cathedral: the Tenneco Health and Fitness Center. Employees ranging from the lowliest clerk to the highest corporate executive exchange their office clothes and their diverse social roles for standard gray "Tenneco Health and Fitness Center" T-shirts and shorts. There are saunas and whirlpools in the locker room, racquetball courts, a running track, and an exercise room.

From the balcony, you look down on the weight room, divided into male and female sections. Three women work out on the Nautilus weight machines. An elderly man furiously pedals an exercise bicycle while two attendants take his blood pressure and run other tests. Other gray-clad Tenneco employees line up at the three computer terminals on the long table at one end of the weight room. They insert their magnetized company ID cards and punch in their workouts for the day. Each month, they receive a computer printout listing their exercises for the month and, according to their weight, the total amount of calories they have burned.

"We have almost perfect statistics," says Barbara Roop, one of the nine full-time members of the Health and Fitness Center staff. "We know how many people use the center, who they are, and what they use it for."

"We are trying to build a sense of self-responsibility," adds Mark Landgreen, the young director of the center. "We want to make people feel that this is their thing. That produces a good feeling about Tenneco—that Tenneco cares."

Recently, the center staff has organized an experiment using these computerized statistics to try to demonstrate a direct link between the workers' health and corporate productivity. A computer tracking system will correlate employee use of the center facilities with a cross section of physiological and organizational indicators. What is the relationship between hypertension and, say, absenteeism? Are the most frequent users of the center also Tenneco's best performers as indicated by promotion records and performance evaluations? The hypothesis, says Barbara Roop, is that "keeping morale up, people feeling good about themselves, helps improve productivity." Of course, all personal information is strictly confidential.

Two floors up from the Health and Fitness Center is the complex's executive dining room. Set on the third-floor balcony, it looks out over the tropical garden. Here the crushed-velvet chairs aren't powder-blue but mauve. Lenox china and fresh-cut flowers adorn every table. But lest one forget the overriding purpose of the Tenneco Employee Center, there are the menus at every place setting. The number of calories in each item is prominently displayed on the right. The fried breaded scallops tartar have 250, the House Salad (Bibb lettuce, spinach, tomatoes, shredded eggs, and bay shrimp) a mere 210. And those items on the menu starred with an asterisk are selections from the Pritikin Diet.

But the message of the brave new workplace does not even stop there. This caring corporation is not reserved for those employees lucky enough to work within its benevolent walls; it extends to everyone. For it is being offered as a model for society as a whole and promoted as the central institution of all social life.

"As geographic communities cease to have real social significance for many citizens," Robert Reich has written in one expression of this point of view, "workplaces are becoming the center of social relationships." And "business enterprises are rapidly becoming the central mediating structures in American society." In the particular future Reich envisions, the corporation will take on the dimensions of a miniature society—for example, taking over from government the administration of a wide range of social programs for its employees, including health care, social security, day care, and disability and unemployment benefits. Even more important, the corporation will become the provider of a crucial social identity for its employees and, ultimately, for all members of society. For the brave new workplace promises a world where "all citizens (and their dependents) will become employee members of some business enterprise."

New technology as the harbinger of meaningful work; the corporation conceived, not as an impersonal bureaucracy, but as a caring community; the workplace as a realm of self-fulfillment; business enterprise as the fundamental source of identity in modern society—these are heady claims. Indeed, they are so visionary, so tinged with possibility and marked with the stamp of the future, that they merit the term "utopia." They promise a world where traditional dissatisfactions dissolve in an atmosphere of unity and good feeling, where conflict and division are abolished, and where the ambivalences of modern industrial life disappear behind the glittering facade of a utopian business culture.

That this corporate utopia of the brave new workplace has emerged just now should really be no surprise. For it is the ironic culmination of a decades-long reflection on the place of work in American society. For some thirty years, sociologists and journalists, novelists and social critics have tried to gauge the distance between the promise of work and its reality. They have seen work as a unique social problem threatening the very conception of American democracy.

Daniel Bell's seminal essay "Work and Its Discontents" is an appropriate place to begin, for it sets the tone of much subsequent writing. In 1956, Bell emphasized the fragmentation and dehumanization of work in the modern industrial factory, traced it to the very principles of efficiency at the foundation of industrial society, and predicted the emergence of a rebellion against those principles in

American workplaces. According to Bell, the "revolt against work" had already begun. "It appears in the constant evasion of thought about work," he wrote, "the obsessive reveries while on the job and the substitution of the glamor of leisure for the drudgery of work." At times, this revolt even passed into action in "crazy racings against the clock to vary the deadly monotony" of the assembly line, in "slowdowns" which he termed "the silent war against production standards," and, "most spectacularly," in "the violent eruptions of wildcat strikes."

Three years later in 1959, the novelist and social critic Harvey Swados echoed Bell's concerns and charged American society with a systematic denial of what he termed the "problem of work." In an article entitled "Work as a Public Issue," in the *Saturday Review,* Swados charged the "growing white collar classes" with refusing to admit "the possibility that millions of American workers may in truth be horribly discontented with their jobs." To do so "would disturb the comfortable mass-media concept of America as a land of blissful togetherness" and "do violence to their own self-esteem." And yet, Swados had to admit that critics such as he and Bell were still in the minority. He lamented "the terrible breadth of the chasm that separates those who *think* from those who *do,* those who *ponder* problems of power from those who *wield* power."

A decade later, the latent workplace rebellion identified by Bell flared up with increasing visibility. Events such as the 1974 wildcat strike at the General Motors assembly plant in Lordstown, Ohio, undermined the media myth of "blissful togetherness," replacing it with images of "blue collar blues" and "white collar woes." And Studs Terkel's best-selling book *Working* documented what he, like Bell, termed the "violence" of working life and the revolt brewing in the American workplace, and gave that rebellion flesh and blood and the discontented worker a voice.

In 1974, a special report to Elliot Richardson, then secretary of health, education, and welfare, endorsed the criticisms of work articulated over the years by Bell, Swados, Terkel, and others. The authors of *Work in America* condemned the "anachronistic authoritarianism" reigning in most American workplaces; predicted that, in a rapidly changing society, such heavy-handed methods would prove counterproductive; and called for an "atmosphere of social experimentation" in which the wholesale redesign of the American workplace could be undertaken. It was as if Swados's dream—work considered as a public issue—had come true.

Today, the preoccupation with work has returned to center stage once again—only this time with some important differences. Whereas earlier reflections about work took place during a period of relative prosperity, the current debate is occurring in an atmosphere of economic uncertainty and even crisis. The almost desperate search for new paths to economic success—perhaps best symbolized by the recent fascination with "Japanese management"—has made the problem of work less a social issue than a matter of industrial competitiveness and economic survival. And where earlier observers of working life tended to view the corporation as an obstacle to reform, today more and more see it as the primary vehicle for social change.

The allure of the brave new workplace is that it promises a wholesale transformation of working life precisely when we seem to need it the most. When the legitimacy and effectiveness of traditional forms of corporate power and practice have been worn thin by the simultaneous impacts of rapid social, economic, and technological change, here is a brand-new model of corporate life promising to reconcile equity with efficiency, meaningful work with high technology, worker satisfaction with corporate profit, and social renewal with economic prosperity.

It is precisely these claims that this book is meant to question. The brave new workplace is certainly a response to past criticisms and present uncertainties. But far from resolving the problems of work, it tends to disguise them, suppress them, and in the process create new problems (as yet unrecognized, let alone understood) even more difficult to address. For this corporate utopia for work denies the essential fact that work in America is a relationship of unequal power, that conflicts of interest are endemic to working life, and that this new model of the corporation, much like the old, is founded on the systematic denial of influence and control to the large majority of working Americans.

Thus, when technology is linked to the imperatives of corporate control, work often becomes the antithesis to the realm of freedom that the image of Charlie Chaplin before the personal computer suggests. Part One examines the managerial assumptions and values motivating the use of new computer technology in many workplaces today; the contradictions for both workers and the corporation itself when managers try to put those assumptions into practice; and the psychological costs of those contradictions for the workers who experience them.

At first glance, the promise of community, as expressed in the image and reputation of the high-tech firms of Silicon Valley, would seem to be a way out of these contradictions of control. But to the degree that it ignores the conflicting interests and unequal power shaping most workplaces today, it can become the foundation for new forms of exploitation and social domination. Part Two shows how recent attempts by the corporation to "humanize" technology and work are fundamentally flawed and how the ideas behind the new management styles gaining popularity in the business community, far from encouraging self-development, can engender a new kind of dependence on corporate power. Using an example from Silicon Valley itself, Part Two also demonstrates how even the most utopian of American corporations refuse to cede to workers some fundamental rights of working life—in this case, occupational safety and health.

Finally, the elevation of the brave new workplace to the position of dominant social institution in American society also has its price: the deterioration of other institutions which, historically, have mitigated the worst effects of the corporate control of work. Part Three charts the impact of the brave new workplace on the most important of these institutions, American trade unionism, and considers the first tentative efforts of unions to address the issues of technology and work that the emergence of the brave new workplace has raised. Part Three and the book as a whole end with an argument abut how to address the continuing inequalities of power shaping working life by creating new institutions dedicated to the social control of technology and work.

The story of the brave new workplace is ultimately abut politics—although not in the narrow way that term is usually understood. It is the most recent chapter in the long struggle between two conflicting conceptions of work and society.

One is the heir to a basic tenet of traditional capitalism—that work is essentially a private affair and that the only institution with the expertise and the legitimacy to shape it is the private corporation. This was the unquestioned premise on which the company towns of early industrial capitalism were built. It was the justification for what one social historian has called the "tyranny of the foreman" in the early mass-production industries. Even after the advent of industrial unionism, it survived in a modified form in the concept of "management prerogatives" still found in most labor contracts today. And it has found its most recent reincarnation in the antiunion, antigovernment, antipublic ideology of contemporary conservatism exemplified by the Reagan administration.

The other conception has been the guiding force of workplace conflict and protest throughout the twentieth century—the idea that work is a public activity far too important to the health of American democracy to be left to the corporation alone. The first efforts at work regulation around the turn of the century, the industrial union movement of the 1930s, and the most recent wave of occupational health and safety and environmental legislation in the 1960s and 1970s all emerged from this same principle. They are part of the ongoing effort to create institutions that represent the public interest at work.

Its reassertion of the primacy of the corporation over working life and its parallel devaluation of the public dimension of work make the brave new workplace a characteristically capitalist utopia. And, today, that utopia seems to have the imprimatur of the future and the affinity of extraordinary promise. The premise of this book is that this future is bankrupt and its promises false—and that the brave new workplace is sowing the seeds of new social conflicts at work and creating the conditions for alternative visions of working life.

PART ONE

THE COMPUTERIZATION OF WORK

CHAPTER ONE

MANAGERIAL VISIONS

THE HUSH OF AN EXECUTIVE OFFICE is interrupted by the soft click of fingers on a VDT keyboard and the staccato sound of a high-speed printer spitting ink onto a page. On an automobile assembly line, spot-welding robots eerily dip and sway in a finely choreographed electronic ballet. White-coated workers load stacks of silicon wafers in the antiseptic atmosphere of a climate-controlled "clean room." In the dim light of an industrial design department, engineers peer at the multicolored images taking shape on their terminal screens.

These are just a few of the many familiar scenes signaling the comprehensive computerization of work. As American business spends $50 billion every year on new workplace technologies, this computerization is causing a major transformation of working life.

Word processing, electronic mail, advanced telecommunications, and other computer-based systems have inaugurated a new era of "office automation." According to SRI International, there are some 1.5 million electronic work stations currently in place in American offices; by 1990 they should multiply more than tenfold to 17.5 million. And the work of one out of every four white-collar workers will take place before their incandescent glow. In the factory, industrial robots, computer-controlled machine tools, even entire "computer-aided" design and manufacturing systems are the components of the most important reorganization of manufacturing work since the arrival of the assembly line more than seventy years ago: "computer-integrated manufacturing."

But computerization is doing something more than merely bringing new tools to the workplace. It is reinventing American industry itself. Most noticeable are the glamorous new high-technology industries—the semiconductor manufacturers, computer companies, and advanced telecommunications firms that provide the building blocks for this computerization of work. Intel Corporation's Robert Noyce calls them "jewels of American innovation." Some observers predict they will be the motor of the U.S. economy of the future, much as the auto and steel industries were in the past. On a well-publicized visit to Boston's high-technology corridor, the President of the United States christened them the "great hope" of the American economy. "I've had the privilege of looking into America's future," beamed an enthusiastic Ronald Reagan, "and the future looks good."

But America's more traditional manufacturing firms are making sure they aren't left behind. General Motors, for example, is not only using industrial robots on its assembly lines; in 1982, GM announced a joint venture with the Japanese robot manufacturer Fujitsu-Fanuc to build and market robots as well. And during the past two years, GM has spent nearly $8 billion to acquire both the Dallas-based Electronic Data Systems Corporation and the Hughes Aircraft Company in a major move into the computer services and high-technology electronics industries.

Or consider General Electric, which spent $2 billion in 1980 alone to modernize its own factories. Since then, GE has spent at least another billion dollars acquiring dozens of small, technology-based companies with expertise at every step of the factory-automation process, as part of a long-term corporate strategy to make GE one of the major providers of the "factory of the future" to manufacturing concerns all over the world.

In the fast-growing service sector, computerization is contributing to the merger of heretofore distinct industries. Retail firms like Sears are buying up financial marketing organizations such as Dean-Witter. Bank holding companies like New York's Citicorp are moving into securities and insurance. The comments of a Citibank vice-president give some of the flavor of this revolutionary change. "The traditional bank was a custodian of cash," he told me. "But now, money is turning into electrons. And banking, just like everything else, is turning into an information-processing business."

As AT&T moves from telecommunications into computers and

information services, as IBM manufactures not only personal computers but also industrial robots, some experts see the emergence of one enormous "Information Economy" that could be a $400 billion business by the end of the 1980s.

Precisely because these changes are so visible, there is a significant feature of this computerization of work that the changes tend to obscure. Behind what appears to be the triumphant and seemingly automatic progress of the new workplace technologies lies a host of invisible yet vitally important *human* assumptions. In a book entitled *The Culture of Technology,* the British science writer Arnold Pacey has written about seeing technology "not only as comprising machines, techniques, and crisply precise knowledge, but also as involving characteristic patterns of organization and imprecise values." In order to understand what the computerization of work means for workers requires penetrating behind technology's visible screen to the attitudes and assumptions, the ideals and "imprecise values" of the people responsible for managing new technology in the brave new workplace today.

Who are these people? They are manufacturing engineers and systems analysts, information systems experts and outside technology consultants. They plan new work systems, design or choose the technology to be used in them, and oversee its implementation in the workplace. While not exactly a clearly defined profession, they do constitute a unique occupational subculture with its own traditions, perspectives, and professional common sense. Call it the realm of the "technology managers," a growing new management class in the brave new workplace.

When we explore it, we are immediately confronted by a curious fact. While the technology of the computer and its arrival in the workplace are themselves relatively new, the ideas about work organization, human motivation, and social purpose currently shaping the use of technology at work are surprisingly old. The computerization of work may indeed constitute a "great hope," but for these technology managers it means something considerably more than new tools, new products and markets, or even newfound economic success. It is nothing less than the welcome realization of an ideal that has tempted industrial managers throughout much of the twentieth century—a captivating image of the workplace as a realm of perfect control. And armed with their chosen instrument, the computer, they are determined, if not to eliminate, then to render harmless the intractable imperfections of human work once and for all.

Young, bright, extremely ambitious; as Steve Taylor puts it, "I'm on a fast track." Twenty-seven years old, a graduate of the University of Michigan Business School, and a certified public accountant, Taylor is currently the executive assistant to the president of a major Houston bank holding company. However, we meet to talk about his previous job, when Taylor traveled the country as a systems analyst and office automation consultant for the Management Information Consulting Division of Arthur B. Andersen & Co., a prominent Chicago management consulting firm.

"There's a lot of room for computer consultants out there," Taylor begins. "It's a *big* business, let me tell you." As new workplace technologies proliferate, and as more and more companies see in them the solution to their productivity problems, corporate managers are turning to technology consultants like Taylor for organizational models, implementation plans, and advice. Such expertise does not come cheap—"no reputable consulting firm will do a feasibility study for less than $30,000 to $50,000," says Taylor, and supervising the actual implementation of a new system can cost twice as much. Nevertheless, technology consultants are in high demand. For what they have to sell is as important as technology itself—an idea and an approach for its use at work. Steve Taylor puts it this way: "Computer systems are just a way to expand management control."

Taylor's comment brings to mind another corporate manager with the same last name—Frederick Winslow Taylor, the turn-of-the-century mechanical engineer, management consultant, and founder of American "scientific management." Like his contemporary namesake, he was living during a period of enormous change at work. The small workshops and family-owned enterprises that had typified nineteenth-century industrialism were giving way to larger corporations. New immigrants were pouring into America's industrial workplaces. As factories grew larger and as the personal bonds of loyalty and dependence that had often linked the worker to the boss in the small firm were erased by the impersonality of the big corporation, the question of how managers were to retain control over work became urgent. Taylor's solution was to replace the personal authority (whether charismatic or coercive) of the traditional boss with an objective "science" of management. Taylorism, as it came to be known, was based on the radical separation of the execution and performance of work from its design. The organization of work was entrusted to a new school of men trained in the techniques of scientific management. They divided jobs into their smallest possible components, easy-to-learn "specialities" to be mastered by the unthinking worker. They performed time and motion studies on those fragments of work to determine "objective" work standards and quotas. Finally, they strived to routinize and standardize work in order to realize that uniform "one best way" of working that would simultaneously guarantee economic efficiency and management control. In his magnum opus, *The Principles of Scientific Management,* first published in 1915, Taylor espoused the principle that would become the unquestioned orthodoxy of American management for more than a generation. "In the past," he wrote, "man has been first; in the future, the system must be first."

Seventy years later, the principles of Taylorism are alive and well in the assumptions of many technology managers. Indeed, one might even say that they are giving Taylor's idea of a dominant "system" new substance by building it into the hardware and software of computer-based work systems. Whereas Taylor wanted to subordinate man to this system, his successors today see computer technology, first and foremost, as a means to eliminate, or at least minimize, the human element in work. Just as Taylor called for the thorough standardization and routinization of tasks, they see computerization as a mechanism to spread that systematic standardization into areas of the workplace and industries where it has rarely been seen before. They also share Taylor's fascination with measurement, and they are using the computer's vast information-processing capabilities to measure and monitor work more intricately and more closely. Finally, by arrogating the design and implementation of new technology to themselves, they are taking the separation of execution and design inherent in Taylorism to a new level.

Of course, since the dawn of the Industrial Revolution, businesses have strived to replace human labor with machines. It should be no surprise that, at its simplest level, using the computer to expand managerial control means getting rid of the human element in work. Using technology as a tool for job elimination in order to cut labor costs is a prominent theme in the way technology managers talk about their jobs. They call it "cleaning up the work process" or "getting rid of excess heads." Steve Taylor says that "our job was eliminating people. In fact, that's the way we had to justify our fee. We always had to be thinking, 'How many people can we get rid of? How can we get the paperwork through faster?' The whole thrust of office automation is to reduce the workforce"—Taylor estimates by about 20 to 30 percent—"in one fell swoop."

A "human factors" supervisor at Bell Labs in Holmdel, New Jersey, Judith Reitman, also reflects this major goal. "There are a lot of places in the Bell System where things cost money," she says, "and the biggest cost is people." Reitman says that of the many ways to cut those costs, the most important is "replacing a piece of the person with something automatic." For illustration, she describes a recent technological innovation that has begun to appear in Bell operating companies around the country known as the Audio Response System. It is a computerized voice synthesizer that provides a caller with assistance in obtaining the number he or she is seeking. When the caller gives an individual's name and address to the directory assistance operator, the operator types the information into the computer, pushes a "green key," then disconnects and lets the computer take over from there. The computer locates the name in its data banks and provides the proper number to the customer (twice, just in case it's missed the first time around).

"There are some 40,000 directory assistance operators out there," explains Reitman. "To shave even one second off the average call can save $24 million a year." The computer-generated voice can eliminate an average of five seconds per call. The faster an operator can complete each call, the sooner she is available for the next. The more calls she can squeeze into her shift, the less operators you need. "You just don't need as many people that way," says Reitman.

Examples like these of "replacing a piece of the person with something automatic" are easy to understand. The computer voice replaces a few seconds of the operator's time. An industrial robot replaces the human movements of a worker on an assembly line. What is harder to grasp is the capacity of the computer to eliminate the need for mental as well as manual labor, to capture not only the actions of work but its internal logic as well. But it is precisely this quality that distinguishes it from previous workplace technologies and allows it to eliminate the human element in work at higher and higher levels of the occupational hierarchy.

A Ph.D. in mechanical engineering, John Eskesen is manager of technical and management information systems at General Electric's Steam Turbine-Generator Operation in Lynn, Massachusetts, where he is responsible for computer-integrated manufacturing and a variety of computerized factory management and information systems. Recently, Eskesen's major concern has been to automate the very first steps in the steam turbine production process—turbine design and drafting.

"If you really want to attack productivity in an engineering organization," explains Eskesen, "the greatest opportunity is the elimination of manual drafting. That's where the major consumption of time is and where the greatest potential gains are." Drafters translate the conceptual designs of an engineer into detailed working drawings which can be used by shop operations to fabricate, machine, and assemble the manufactured product. At Lynn, John Eskesen is automating this detail drafting work.

In most industries, the usual first step in the automation of drafting is to replace the manual drafting board with a computerized "interactive graphics system." "Structured" components are predesigned and stored in the computer system's graphics library; then, complex composite "pictures" are created "interactively" by drafters working at video screens. For example, the drawing of a large turbine casing casting, which took over three hundred hours to produce on a drafting board, takes only eighty hours on an interactive graphics system, using the information stored in the system's computers.

The ultimate step, however, is to transcend this interactive method altogether. By means of a computer program that replicates the logic of the layout work process, the software generates the same drawing information automatically. "The savings are enormous," says Eskesen. "The same casing drawing which took eighty hours to produce on the interactive system can now be done without any human interaction at all in a matter of minutes on a minicomputer."

Because of the ability of the computer to eliminate the need for large quantities of previously manual work, "this whole business of automation has become a sensitive issue," says Eskesen, "especially among our drafting personnel." He pauses, searching for the right words to make his own position perfectly clear. "Don't misunderstand me, I'm not advocating the abolition of drafting," he says. "Drafting is an honorable profession and we'll always need creative draftsmen to work on prototype designs. All I'm suggesting is that the mundane and repetitive detail work, for which fairly precise rules usually exist, will be done entirely by computer."

Nevertheless, to Eskesen, the overall implications of computerized automation are clear. "There's no question that people's jobs are in jeopardy. In engineering, in drafting, and throughout industry, the computer will continue to replace repetitive clerical-type work. Naturally people are going to object; it's only natural. They would like security. Who wouldn't? The fact is, no one has that luxury today unless one happens to be a tenured university professor."

Of course, whether or not the elimination of certain jobs by new computer technology constitutes an unemployment problem for society as a whole is extremely difficult to tell with any certainty. Technology is only one of many factors determining the aggregate unemployment rate. Short-term business cycles, shifts in the strength of various industries, levels of imports and exports, even long-term demographic trends may all be equally or even more important. While new technology certainly eliminates some jobs, it creates new ones as well. And the potential of new technology to make individual firms more competitive means that, in specific cases, technology can actually save certain jobs.

And yet, what is to ensure that the jobs created by new technology will make up for those it eliminates? And even if there is no overall employment crisis, what are the institutional mechanisms to guarantee that those workers most affected by technological displacement—middle-aged manufacturing workers, say, or the women who by a vast majority occupy the lower rungs of the occupational ladder in the service sector—will have the skills and the training to shift to other jobs? And what, if anything, should we do about the social paradox best expressed by a May 1983 declaration of the Business Council (a prestigious business lobbying group made up of some of the nation's top corporate executives), which announced that advanced automation was a key corporate strategy for economic recovery but because of the labor-saving advantages of this technology, many of their employees laid off during the recession would not be called back to work?

Among economists and public policy-makers, these are questions of enormous controversy. Among technology managers themselves, they are rarely considered. One manager who has thought about them is Tony Friscia, a consultant on the "factory of the future" at the Yankee Group, a Boston management consulting firm. "It's only a gut feeling," says Friscia, "and I don't really have any statistics to back it up. But there's got to be a five-to-ten-year period, probably around 1985 to 1995, when there are going to be a lot of victims. Because there are certain people whom you're just not going to retrain. What is the guy who's fifty years old and spent the last twenty years in some factory going to do? You're not going to train him to be a robotics technician; for the most part, you want young guys for that."

Friscia has no answer to his question. "Ultimately, those who survive, survive, and those who don't, don't. I guess that's the capitalist way of looking at things. In theory, it makes a lot of sense. Maybe even in practice, when you look at things over the long term, it makes sense. But if I were a labor negotiator, the fundamental issue for me would be 'How are you going to save the people I'm responsible for?' Or, if I were a legislator, I'd want to be damn sure that there weren't going to be so many people uncared for that I was setting myself up for some kind of social upheaval. A society just can't survive when a substantial portion of the population is out of work."

But Tony Friscia is something of an exception. Few technology managers are so reflective about the social implications of their work. The simple reason is that they don't have to be. While the corporation enjoys the benefits of labor-saving technology, it can avoid most of the costs by "externalizing" them onto society as a whole. Far more typical are the comments of a Citibank executive whom I interviewed.

"There's a question for society in all this," he told me. "What happens to those people who can't make it in this superefficient world that we're creating? It's true; over the long run, fewer people will work at Citibank. Who knows? Maybe we'll all work a twenty-hour week. But that's not our problem; that's up to society to decide."

Another goal of scientific management was to standardize work, on the theory that the more routine and predictable a particular production process, the easier it would be to control. As with the elimination of manual and mental labor, computerization takes standardization to a new level.

In manufacturing, there has traditionally been a trade-off between standardization and flexibility. On one side, there is the familiar example of the assembly line. Ever since Henry Ford first installed it in his Hamtramck, Michigan, factory in 1913, it has been the archetype of modern mass production. Ford's assembly line was the culmination of nearly one hundred years of technological development. The MIT social scientist Charles Sabel writes, "It was as if the Ford engineers, putting in place the crucial pieces of a giant jigsaw puzzle, suddenly made intelligible the major themes of a century of industrialization."

The traditional assembly line is predicated on the comprehensive standardization of parts and the routinization of production. It consists of highly specialized "dedicated" machinery and narrowly defined jobs. When machines are matched to workers in a highly codified work process, the result is an elaborate control of production. But the assembly line is also rigid and inflexible. Its much-vaunted efficiency depends on high-volume production and the existence of stable mass markets. If demand is chronically low or subject to rapid oscillations or sudden shifts, then the assembly line, difficult to adapt to changing circumstances, is not worth the massive investments necessary to install it in the first place. Likewise, the mechanization of certain tasks along the assembly line (the term "automation" was first coined in Detroit in the late 1940s to describe it) has been as rigid as the assembly line itself, suitable for only a small minority of radically simplified unchanging tasks, islands of mechanized automation in a sea of manual factory work.

Because of this inflexibility, mass production has always been accompanied by another form of industrial organization—batch manufacturing. Nearly 75 percent of American manufacturing today consists of products that are not amenable to standardization, either because their markets are too small or too volatile or because their components are too complex. In batch manufacturing plants, work is organized to maximize flexibility. Workers use general-purpose machinery (lathes, milling machines, and other machine tools) to produce many different products or parts in relatively small quantities. What batch manufacturing gains in flexibility, however, it loses in predictability and control. And it has gone virtually untouched by earlier and clumsier forms of automation.

However, computerization promises to bridge the gap between flexibility, on the one hand, and standardization and control, on the other. It can provide industrial managers with what one engineer described to me as "the best of both worlds." An appropriate example is the turbine design work process at General Electric in Lynn.

Each turbine that GE manufactures is like a custom-made piece of clothing, designed to match the unique requirements of a particular customer. To create each turbine design has demanded both a highly skilled workforce of engineers and drafters and a flexible work process.

From the moment an order is placed, a design engineer begins working to capture the agreed-upon specifications (known as the turbine's "steam conditions") in a digital "design summary"—a kind of mathematical picture of what the turbine looks like. Traditionally, this design information was then passed on to a senior designer (the highest-skilled drafter) who translated the "engineering" design into a drawing of the turbine's "steam path." The steam path, says John Eskesen, is "the guts of the turbine, and this steam path layout is the single most important document we create. It defines the basic internal structure of the turbine. And all the drawings of the turbine's components are derived from it."

To a large extent, the senior designer's task of creating the steam-path layout is what Eskesen calls "conceptual work." Traditionally, many of the engineering rules governing this step in the design process were informal; layout definition was left to the skill of the individual designer. "The senior designer is conceptualizing," he explains. "Some of the rules are well defined; some are not. You can be sure that if you give two senior designers a steam path layout, you'll end up with two different designs."

Manually producing a steam-path layout used to take about six weeks. Upon its completion, lesser-skilled drafters would create increasingly more detailed layouts of the turbine casing, rotor, buckets, nozzles, and "labyrinth seals" within the turbine. On the whole, this work is less "conceptual" than that of the senior designer; Eskesen calls it more "mundane." And yet, even these more basic forms of drafting work required considerable skill and allowed drafters substantial flexibility. "Drafting personnel at all levels are given a fair degree of design freedom," says Eskesen. "When they look at a component within the steam turbine and see that it's not quite what they want, they design something else, and add it to the drawing inventory."

As long as turbines were designed and layouts drafted manually, standardization was difficult to control. Before the computer, says Eskesen, "the vast amount of information needed to support standardization was just too hard to manage." To routinize the procedures would have destroyed the flexibility necessary to ensure high quality.

With the capacity of the computer to manage and manipulate vast quantities of data, however, new levels of standardization are possible without losing the flexibility of the traditional design process. "Generally speaking," says Eskesen, "almost all the detail work can be made to follow hard and fast rules laid down by engineering.

Since these rules can be translated into computer language, it's relatively straightforward for the computer to do the job. The days when different drafters produced different layouts from the same design information are gone." Moreover, by carefully organizing this standardization of design information at the level of the turbine "sub-elements," computerization can greatly increase the flexibility of the overall design process as well—what might be termed "flexible standardization."

In a sense, the flexibility that was once the possession of the drafter is now transferred to the system itself. "Computers make the process very rigorous," says Eskesen. "Design freedom at the level of nonprototype elements is at odds with the discipline which a computer system requires and tries to enforce. If a drafter takes a piece of information and puts it into the system, the information has got to be right." Any variance from specified procedures "will send shock waves that proceed right through the entire system."

For the most part, Eskesen confines his comments about standardization to "mundane," low-level drafting tasks. "It's technically difficult and usually not economically feasible to have computers do conceptual work," he says. However, when it comes to the steam-path layout prepared by the senior designer, in a sense, he and his management team have done precisely that. "We've figured out how to program the logic of the design rules into the computer," says Eskesen. The result is an "expert system" in which the engineer's digital summary of the turbine design feeds directly into a program that generates a steam-path layout in less than a minute. The information is then automatically fed to a series of more detailed drawing programs, which define the details for fabrication and machining of the casing, rotor, and various internal turbine elements.

"In the not too distant future," Eskesen claims, "an engineer will sit down at a design computer terminal, take the basic customer information, and just punch the numbers in. Then, the computer will automatically generate all the design, drafting, planning, and machining data and all the capacity planning information necessary to effectively load the machines in the shops." In fact, Eskesen has already linked some of his design programs with those used to instruct computer-controlled machine tools how to machine the mammoth turbine parts on the Lynn shop floor.

Eskesen even imagines a day when layouts and drawings, fixtures of industrial life for centuries, will become obsolete. After all, he muses, "in the computerized workplace, drawings are generally superfluous. They're just documents that allow us to interpret readily what the hell is going on." In the future, perhaps people will learn to read "digital summaries of what turbines look like" painted in the unambiguous colors of the digital computer code.

Standardized work is controllable work. Perhaps the most effective instrument in the Taylorist system of control is the systematic measurement of work by time and motion studies. But whereas the measurement of work under traditional Taylorism was occasional, limited to the visits of the time-study specialists, the computer's vast information-processing capacity allows technology managers to extend the monitoring of production over time, making it constant. They talk about increasing the "visibility" of work—as if computer screens were windows peering into the heart of the brave new workplace.

Since graduating from MIT in 1979, Joe Kracunas has been designing and installing a direct numerical control (DNC) machining system at GE's Aircraft Engine Group in Lynn. The DNC system links sixty computer-controlled machine tools to a central computer. Programs to run the tools are loaded in the host computer in a bright white air-conditioned control room, then electronically transferred to each individual machine out on the shop floor. DNC is a major part of the computerization of factory work, because it ties each individual machine into a factory-wide system. What's more, it allows management to track machine performance with a comprehensiveness never before achieved. "With this new system," explains the twenty-seven-year-old Kracunas, "you can monitor every machine out there in the shop. The real payback is in factory management and control."

In effect, DNC creates an information network on the factory floor. Just as information is sent to the machines and operators on the shop floor—for example, part programs and machining instructions—it is also extracted from them. Currently the DNC system at Lynn collects data on machine utilization: how often the machine is cutting parts and at what feed-rate settings. When a particular machine has been turned off for more than fifteen minutes, the computer prompts its operator for an explanation by means of a message displayed on the terminal perched on the top of each machine's control panel. The operator's answer is entered into the machine's utilization record. Planned enhancements include attaching special electronic probes to each machine in order to monitor oil pressure, power supply voltages, servomotor outputs, and other indicators of machine performance. "We want to attach sensors to different parts of the tool," says Kracunas, "sort of to monitor its health." At some point in the not too distant future, the DNC system at Lynn will be so sophisticated that every time someone comes to fix a malfunctioning machine, he will arrive with a computer printout detailing the machine's current status and entire performance history.

Early in 1984, Kracunas installed a feature he first saw at another GE facility. At the front of the control room , hanging from the ceiling, a large video screen displays a map of all the machines on the shop floor. Every machine is one of three colors: those running smoothly are bright green; those momentarily turned off are yellow; and those "down" for maintenance are a flashing red.

Another example of these electronic windows looking into the brave new workplace is a computer system called manufacturing resource planning, or MRP. MRP concerns itself with factory scheduling and inventory control, some of the most costly problems in industry. Nearly 85 percent of the time that a part is in a factory, it is simply waiting for something to happen to it—waiting to begin a production run, waiting to move from one machine to the next, or simply waiting to be shipped out to the customer once it is finished and packed. The average machine tool spends only 6 percent of its available time actually cutting metal, for example. The cost of inventory buildup is enormous. Half the space in the average factory serves as a warehouse—parts sitting around. One of the thorniest challenges for most manufacturers is how to set up a system for the continuous flow of parts through the workplace.

MRP systems are complex computer programs which do just that. They work backward from the delivery date of a factory's products, in order to orchestrate an elaborate schedule of raw materials, machine time, tools, labor, and other resources. They define the precise interactions between each component from the beginning to the end of a nonstop production process. Ideally, raw materials are delivered on the very day they are to be used, then travel from one machining process to another in an uninterrupted flow across the factory floor. More than a hundred such MRP systems have been developed and put to use in more than ten thousand manufacturing sites. Some of the companies that use them have been able to cut back their inventories by as much as 40–50 percent.

It would be hard to overestimate how excited this can make technology managers. "MRP is not just a computer system; it's a whole new management philosophy," one told me. "At our plant, we treat MRP like a religion," says another. Tony Friscia, from the Yankee Group, describes the implications: "If something breaks down, the office *immediately* knows about it," he says. "If there is an inventory need, the office is *immediately* notified. When you have access to all that information, then your ability to manage improves significantly. You can eliminate all the paper passing back and forth from hand to hand. You don't have to wait until tomorrow or next Monday morning for an update on your inventories or your production runs. You've got it *now*. That's what they mean when they talk about improving management control."

Such intricate control of work is admirable when applied to machines or products moving through a shop or factory. But what about when it is applied to people? It does not take long to realize that when the managers of the brave new workplace talk about expanding managerial control, they mean control over workers as well as over products or machines. Here, the legacy of Taylorism reaches its most dangerous expression.

At one point during a long conversation about the computerization of work in the banking industry, a vice-president at a Citicorp subsidiary passes a large computer printout across the expanse of his desk. It is an MIS Daily Operating Report for a clerk in the firm's Chicago office. MIS stands for Management Information System, and it is key software in any office automation package. With it, managers can correlate large quantities of information about work-flows and performance—even in offices hundreds of miles away. This particular clerk's printout indicates the percentage of his (or, perhaps, her) day spent on the telephone and that spent processing records of the financial services the firm provides. It compares the time it took the clerk to complete each item with a standard time allocated by Citicorp industrial engineers. The manager explains that a good productivity rating would be in the neighborhood of 91 percent. On this particular day, the clerk's is a feeble 38.8. "If I were the manager there, I would want to know why," he says, in passing.

The MIS report also lists the clerk's "utilization" rate—the por-tion of the day spent actually processing forms. Multiplying the pro-ductivity and utilization ratios, says the manager, gives an overall "operating index," an "all-inclusive measure" of performance. Fi-nally, the MIS form reports this clerk's "backlog," item by item (those processing jobs in the computer yet to be completed). Each day the system automatically "ages" the items, so managers can pin-point workers with an insufficiently rapid "turnaround."

"We monitor productivity on a daily basis," explains the Citi-corp vice-president. "The system lists every clerk, every day. It tells us the work he got in and the work he got out." He pauses, lifting the printout off the desk for emphasis. "And we can get one of these for every work station in the business."

The use of technology as an instrument of control not only over work processes but over the people who perform them is nowhere more clear than in the way technology managers talk about their own jobs managing the design and implementation of computer sys-tems in the brave new workplace. Where Frederick Taylor divided the organization of work (reserved to the initiates of scientific man-agement) from its execution (left to workers), they are applying this principle to technology itself. How these designers of the brave new workplace treat the "users" of new technology is a case study in the expanding corporate control of work. At its worst, it is little more than an exercise in manipulation.

The consulting job that Steve Taylor remembers most vividly is the computerization of an office at Texas International Airlines in Houston, now a part of Continental Airlines. He was sent by the Chicago office of Arthur B. Andersen to design and implement what he calls a "work measurement and performance evaluation system" in the company's revenue accounting department. Some 130 clerks, mostly women, performed various processing jobs in the office: they priced tickets, tabulated the amounts on passenger coupons from Texas International flights, and did some fifteen other clerical tasks. Taylor's job was to create a computer system that would automatically monitor their work, record their output, and calculate their productivity by means of a mathematical index.

According to Taylor, his work at Texas International was a classic example of the technology consulting process. The first step was to meet with company executives. "Any computer consultant works for top management," he explains. "You come into the corporation, sit down with upper management, and help them decide what they want. It's a top-down approach. Top management gives us the mantle, and we truck on down to the workplace and put their directives into effect."

At Texas International, top management expressed the usual desires for increased productivity, for people to work, in Taylor's phrase, "faster, smarter, and better." But corporate executives also expressed another concern. Clerks in the office had recently voted to join the Teamsters union. The "performance evaluation" system was management's way of showing them that it was still in charge.

Receiving the go-ahead from top management, however, was only the first step in a long, carefully planned procedure. Next, Taylor had to move to the workplace itself. "If you're going to do a study, you've got to have information, right?" Before he could rationalize the revenue accounting office, he needed to know precisely how the office clerks did their work. And the best source for that information was the clerks themselves.

At this stage, says Taylor, a key role is played by middle management. "Middle management's place is to decide how to break it to the employees," he says. Taylor held meetings with office supervisors to discuss this delicate problem. Finally, someone suggested, "Let's tell them this is 'methods improvement.'" The announcement was made that an outside consultant was "going to help you do a better job."

Thus, the accounting clerks at Texas International were neither surprised nor concerned about the appearance of the young stranger in their office, asking questions day after day about their jobs. As Steve Taylor says, with equal parts of amazement and pride, "They didn't know what was going on." Step by step, he began to understand how work was done in the revenue office. He sat down with workers for long intensive interviews probing them on how they did their jobs. Unbeknownst to the clerks, he was also analyzing their descriptions and redesigning the work process from scratch. "You determine what's good, what they should be doing, and what can be automated." Having formulated a plan to streamline office work, he then began slowly to introduce it to the workforce. He suggested new work procedures and started timing workers as they did their jobs. "Slowly but surely," he says, "we're going to teach them something that outlives us."

Of course, the rationalization of the revenue accounting office did not always proceed smoothly. For one thing, the fiction of "methods improvement" had to be maintained at all costs, and at times Taylor felt as if he were on a psychological and emotional roller coaster. "After a while," he says, "an awful lot of people kind of suspected that something was different" about the way they were doing their jobs, different in a way they didn't particularly like. But for Taylor, this only added to the excitement and challenge of his own. "I loved it when I worked on that job," he recalls fondly. "It was always so crazy because it was so political." The wrong word to the wrong person and "you could really get burned. Because then, the whole scheme would be off."

Fortunately for Taylor, he succeeded in maneuvering his way through the different groups in the office without blowing his cover. Now he was ready for the final step of the work rationalization process—the creation of the actual computer system. The computer integrated productivity data from the various jobs the clerks performed. It could be programmed to produce reports on individuals or on the office as a whole on a monthly, weekly, or even daily basis. The reports listed how many items in each category a particular clerk had processed, and tabulated a productivity index rating her overall efficiency. The printout included what Taylor calls "a nifty little trick." It itemized each worker's absences as well. "If they were gone, it would show up on the printout," he says. "You know—'Wednesday, no activity.'"

As soon as the system was up and running, Taylor and the office managers at Texas International noticed a curious phenomenon. Office productivity would dip, like clockwork, at the same two points of every day—around nine in the morning and three in the afternoon. Taylor traced this distressing decline in performance to what he calls "abuses" in the office's flextime system. The clerks had the option of arriving at work anytime between six and nine in the morning. Depending on their hour of arrival, they would leave between three and six in the afternoon. When the last of the office workers arrived at nine, those who had been working since six would stop to say hello. Productivity, says Taylor, would plummet. And when those who had been working since six left at three, the same thing would happen again. "So," says Steve Taylor matter-of-factly, "management decided to cut back on their flextime."

There are moments when the work of technology managers like Steve Taylor sounds almost like a crusade: to eliminate inefficient practices, to pare wasted actions, to squeeze out every second of "dead time" like so many drops from a too-absorbent sponge. Because these changes they are planning for work are so far-reaching (and have such enormous implications for those doing the work), the managers of the brave new workplace also come armed with a promise. It is, of course, a promise of efficiency—that the new workplace technology will ensure competitiveness and guarantee our economic and social prosperity—but it is also a promise about the quality of working life. Put simply, they claim that their computerization of work is going to make for better jobs.

One facet of this claim is that technology will eliminate "dog work," the boring, dirty, dangerous jobs that no one wants to do anyway. Speaking about the computer-generated recording that "replaces a piece of the person with something automatic," Judith

Reitman adds that "this kind of replacement gets the workers very happy. You may be reducing the workforce, but it's for a very tedious job. There are fewer workers but the jobs are much better."

Technology managers also argue that the changes brought about by computerization ultimately have a positive effect on skilled jobs. Thus, after describing the automation of the senior designer's "steam path," John Eskesen argues, "If the logic of design and drafting rules can be programmed into a computer, then by definition, it's unskilled labor. What the computer has done is to take on the repetitive detailing work at many levels of sophistication." It is like a chemical solution that leaches out "mundane" tasks, leaving behind a pure precipitate of ever more challenging and more innovative "conceptual work."

Indeed, many see the capacity of computerization to introduce a kind of "flexible specialization" as the occasion for a total reinvention of work, a reinvention that will result in more integrated and less fragmented jobs and will allow workers to perform more creative, useful, and interesting tasks. "Given the training and the opportunity," says a top technology manager in the auto industry, "most people would like very much to expand the horizons of their jobs." For him, computerization "will broaden the spectrum of worker involvement and allow the individual to input more of his personality into his job."

All these possibilities are potentially true. But when the technology of the computer is conceived primarily as a means for managerial control, the claims of the technology managers are often proved wrong on both counts. The assumption of improved work quality is regularly contradicted in the brave new workplace today. And even the promise of increased efficiency turns out to be far more difficult to achieve than most managers tend to think.

CHAPTER TWO

───────

CONTRADICTIONS OF CONTROL

───────

DAVE BOGGS IS A THIRTY-SIX-YEAR-OLD MACHINIST with a military bearing (the result of his four years in the Air Force) and, until recently, an abiding passion for his job. He works as a sheet metal mechanic for Eastern Airlines in Miami, Florida, where he operates machine tools that translate the blueprints of drafters and engineers into different aircraft parts. "To me," he says, "it's a craft. I've worked hard to get where I'm at." In the last few years, however, Boggs has lost much of his passion for his work. He can fix the date of his estrangement precisely—to December 1979 and the arrival at the Eastern sheet metal fabrication shop of the Strippit 750 Fabricenter, a computer-controlled punch press.

A punch press is a general-purpose machine tool, like a milling machine or a lathe. Traditionally, a machinist sets up and operates such a machine manually, deciding how best to realize the specifications required for each particular part. However, with the advent of small, powerful microprocessors that can be attached to each machine, this process has changed considerably. Through computerization, the precise movements of the machine can be programmed mathematically and encoded on a plastic tape. The tape is read by the machine's programmable controller, which translates its instructions into the movements of the tool. The technical name for this automatic process is computer numerical control, or CNC.

As soon as he learned that his department was getting its first piece of computerized equipment, Boggs immediately volunteered to operate the machine. The idea of computer control appealed to his machinist's sense of perfection. "I like to make parts that are right on the money," he explains. "But no matter how hard you try with a regular punch press, you're always going to be off." For Boggs, the computer promised "a greater degree of accuracy." In his unending quest for the perfect part, it would eliminate the "human mistake factor."

Before the Strippit 750 arrived in the sheet metal shop, the manufacturer offered a free course to train Eastern employees in the programming and operation of the CNC equipment. As one of the three operators selected to run the machine, Boggs looked forward to going. But when he looked for his name on the course list, he found it wasn't there. Two foremen, a tooling engineer, and a draftsman who had recently been transferred to the newly created programming department were selected instead. Boggs was informed that the course was for managers only and that he didn't need to know the skills taught in it.

Closed out from the official training course, Boggs picked up what he could on his own initiative from the Strippit employees sent to install the machine on the shop floor. He and his fellow operators obtained copies of the programming and operating manuals from the Strippit crew, Xeroxed them from cover to cover, and, because it was difficult to find time during the day, took them home and pored over them at night. During the next three months, they worked together to learn the rudiments of programming on the CNC machine's microprocessor. Supplementing their education with a little math and trigonometry, they figured out how to "input" on the keyboard of the machine's control panel. They wrote up practice programs and tried them out on the machine, correcting each other's mistakes as they went along. "We were well on our way to programming," remembers Boggs.

But when the time came actually to begin operating the machine for production, Boggs and the other machinists were excluded from programming work. Sole responsibility for producing the tapes to run on the machine was given to the new programming department. The device for creating the tapes (called a Fabriwriter) was kept there; Boggs had no access to it. He could still input programs manually into the microprocessor attached to the machine, but the computer had a small memory and could carry only one program at a time. Moreover, management canceled an order for an accessory known as a tape interface, which would have allowed the operators to transfer their programs to tape directly at the punch press.

Boggs soon discovered that, these obstacles notwithstanding, he could still create more efficient programs more quickly himself; he did so, and simply read them into the computer's memory, instead of waiting for the tape from the programming department. "Since we understood the machinery and the mathematics involved in making the part," he explains, "we were days and days ahead of the programmer. We could make a program in an hour and a half or two hours that would take him six weeks to do. And sometimes it would take nearly three months for him to get a program to work right."

In order to resolve this log jam, the programming department resorted to the obvious technological solution. Management purchased a computer system that would allow the programmer assigned to the Strippit 750 to produce tapes automatically. The only problem was that its language was not wholly compatible with that of the microprocessor on the machine itself, which meant that any program produced on the new system could not take full advantage of the considerable capabilities of the computerized punch press.

Boggs leafs through the sheaf of papers he brings to our meeting and pulls out a dramatic example of this dilemma. They are two programs for the same part, one created by the Eastern programming department, the other by Boggs on his machine. The department's program makes 65 parts on a 40-by-18-inch sheet of metal, requires 978 blocks of information and a fantail paper tape approximately 250 feet long. It still leaves the parts attached to the sheet by small metal tabs that have to be cut, filed, and sanded after passing through the punch press. Boggs's program, on the other hand, makes 306 parts on the same size sheet, has only 29 blocks of information, and actually blanks out the parts while the sheet is still in the machine—thus dispensing with the boring finishing work. Boggs figures that his program is about 470 percent more efficient than that of the programming department.

Despite such compelling evidence, Boggs and his co-workers faced mounting pressure not only to stop programming the Strippit machine but to help the programmer assigned to it to correct his own mistakes. "What is this?" Boggs remembers asking. "Not only is the guy stealing my job, but I've got to give him the information to do it with? That's like a guy robbing your home and you stand out front with a key saying, 'Here you go, bud, that's it over there.' " After consistently complaining when the programs did not meet certain job specifications, the machine operators stopped receiving the information that allowed them to make that judgment in the first place. At another point, what Boggs calls "deliberately false and misleading statements" were made about the quantity and quality of tapes coming out of the programming department.

Finally, Eastern called the Strippit company back to the sheet metal shop, this time to put an on-off switch on the button used to gain access to the machine's computer memory. The foreman put a lock on the door to the switch and pocketed the key. It was an attempt to put an end to the machinists' programming efforts once and for all. "What they want," says Boggs, "is for the sheet metal mechanic to be someone who just picks out the metal, cuts it to size, puts it in the clamps, and pushes the button, then takes the part out and does it all over again. But the actual layout, which has always been part of our job, is now transferred to them. They've cut off the interest in the machine. Anybody can push a button."

Almost from the moment the Strippit 750 was moved into the sheet metal shop, Dave Boggs mounted a one-man campaign to get permission to program the computer-controlled machine. The way he saw it, the programming was an essential part of the job of effectively operating the new punch press. He complained to his foreman, without much effect. He wrote a letter to the director of Eastern's Aircraft Service Center to protest "the removal of work . . . away from the sheet metal shop and into the hands of draftsmen and engineers." As for the lock on the control panel door, Boggs took a more direct approach. "Along with being a sheet metal mechanic," he says, "I'm also a qualified locksmith." Some of the keys in the sheet metal shop began to fit the Strippit control panel lock although they never had before.

Boggs also filed a grievance with his local of the International Association of Machinists. He wrote a letter to the president of the IAM's District 100, representing Eastern machinists all over the country. At one point, even the union's international headquarters in

Washington got involved, and sent a staff member to interview Boggs. But eventually, "things just settled down to the same old status quo."

Then on May 31, 1981, something happened to convince Boggs that the end of his long struggle was at hand. While getting on an Eastern plane in Atlanta for a return flight to Miami, he saw Eastern Airlines president and former astronaut Frank Borman quickly disappear into first class. Boggs hurriedly scribbled a note ("Are you interested in productivity?" it read; "If you are, I'd like to talk with you") and gave it to a steward to deliver. Within minutes after takeoff, a short blond man in a summer business suit walked back to Boggs's seat and said, "Hello, my name is Frank Borman."

Boggs recounted to his boss the long sorry story of the Strippit 750. He told Borman about the conflicts with the programming department, the missing tape interface, the lock on the END button. He claimed that, if he could just run the machine the way he wanted to, he could produce ten times as many parts in four hours as were currently being done in eight. Borman asked if Boggs had any documentation. The machinist reached into his briefcase and handed the astronaut-turned-business-executive a half-inch stack of letters, grievances, company memoranda, and numerical control programs that he just happened to be carrying with him.

"To tell you the truth," says Boggs, "talking to the man, I thought something was going to be done." For five long months, he waited expectantly, but there was no word. Finally, he paid a visit to Borman's office in Miami to see what was causing the delay, only to learn from the president's secretary that her boss had lost the file. So Boggs prepared and sent off another packet.

A month later, he received a one-page memo in reply. While he thanked the machinist for his concern, Borman claimed that it was in Eastern's "best interest" to have all the programming for the company's numerical control machines done by a "small, specialized group." Moreover, this was "the normal practice" in other industries using the new computerized equipment. Nevertheless, Borman concluded, Boggs could rest assured. Company policy was not intended "to detract from the responsibility or importance of machine operators."

Dave Boggs continues to work at Eastern, but occasionally he takes a part-time job on the side. He has become a freelance programmer for other companies in the Miami area using the Strippit computer-controlled machinery—at a rate of $75 per program.

No one understands better than Boggs how the Taylorist use of new technology contradicts not only many workers' expectations and ambitions for their jobs, but also the promise of the new technology itself. At one point in our conversation, he launches into a paean to the technical virtuosity of the new computer-controlled machine tools. "Really, the jobs are getting a lot more interesting than they were," he says. "It's a grind to sit there and do all that stuff by hand." The problem is the way that the corporation tries to use technology to reorganize how work is done. "They want to cut us completely out of it," says Boggs. The decision not to purchase the tape interface, the sudden absence of key production information, the lock installed on the Strippit's computer console are all effects, not of some impersonal and inevitable "technological change," but of human choices and human power.

Boggs's story also cuts against the grain of our conventional image of industrial workers. To a degree, we are all prisoners of the mechanistic ideology of Taylorism with its view of workers as mere elements of a vast production system. We tend to think of them as irresponsible and uncaring about their work (which then, of course, becomes a justification for eliminating them by technology and automation). As Boggs suggests, *they* don't see things that way. For them, this conflict between the promise of technology and the power of the corporation penetrates to the very core of their sense of themselves and their work.

Consider the example of worker skills. Few aspects of working life are more crucial to a person's sense of mastery in and satisfaction at work, and more important to the long-term success of an organization. How workers acquire skills, what opportunities they have to exercise them, the very quality of the skills they learn and use are at the center of the contradictions of control in the brave new workplace. The new technology managers claim that while the computerization of work renders certain skills obsolete, it allows for more complex skills. The "dog work" of routine manual tasks is replaced by the more conceptual tasks of computerized work. In the abstract, this is true, as Boggs himself perceives. But his own experience cuts across this scenario. For while the Strippit 750 precludes the need for certain manual skills common to his machinist's trade, management blocked him from acquiring and using the new programming skills that accompany computerization. The critics of Taylorism would say that his job has been "deskilled."

The reasonable suggestion has been made that one way for workers to benefit from new technology would be to ensure that they are trained in the skills necessary for its use. On the surface, this suggestion has the compelling persuasiveness of simple common sense. But as the Boggs story tells us, retraining is no simple matter. Like technology itself, it too is caught up in the unequal relations of power at work.

Acquiring new workplace skills is a little like learning how to drive. No matter how many hours of driver's education one has, the real expertise is learned on the road. In the same way, most skills that workers learn are obtained on the job. Corporations have traditionally been hesitant to provide comprehensive on-the-job training, however, since shop-floor education is expensive, and there is little protection against an employee's taking the new skills elsewhere. Formal apprenticeship programs are rare in American industry. Most companies have preferred, when they could, to organize jobs as narrowly as possible in order to minimize training (a key tenet of Taylorism). And when they couldn't, they have relied on the informal organization of workers on the shop floor to provide an environment where people can learn from one another. At Eastern, says Dave Boggs, "they don't supply us with any training. It's up to the people who work with a guy to teach him his job. They rely on the camaraderie of the people to share their knowledge with each other. If you don't know how to do the job, ask the guy at the next bench."

What happens to this arrangement—or nonarrangement—when there is rapid technological change? On the one hand, formal training in new skills becomes all the more important. On the other, the Taylorist emphasis on using technology to fragment jobs and increase managerial control makes that training increasingly difficult for workers to acquire on the job. "With this new machine," Boggs continues, "there was nobody to teach us. We couldn't go to the next bench. We had to learn on our own." And even when workers overcome these obstacles and, like Boggs, pick up the new skills independently, it does little good unless they are given the opportunity to practice them in the course of their work. Thus, worker training and skill acquisition both become hostages to the corporate control of the workplace.

The contradictions of control extend to the very goals of productivity and efficiency that are the ostensible justification of the new workplace technology. At Eastern, the restriction of programming to a management department means less efficient tapes and slower production runs. Management's solution is not to reorganize the work, but to devise an even more elaborate technological quick fix—a new computer for the programmers. Dave Boggs is convinced that "they cost themselves more than it's worth. They are deliberately losing money day after day just in order to maintain control."

But this is not a clear-cut process. Rather, it is the outcome of a complicated and ambiguous struggle. Often the engineers' ideal of control collides with the intractable realities of the shop floor. Despite management's prohibitions, Boggs can still do some programming—for the simple reason that his immediate supervisors realize they would never get the work done otherwise. "Although the machine is computerized," explains Boggs, "it's not infallible. They still can't do without us altogether. We still have some control in there."

Yet, the damage has been done—damage to the individual, damage to the work organization itself. The most tragic outcome, in both human and economic terms, is how this conflict is ruining Dave Boggs's relation to his work. When he describes his job as a "craft," he is talking about something more than skill, training, or efficiency. He means a certain sense of engagement and self-possession, the challenge of learning, a conviction of being "in control" in the broadest sense of that term. His desire to program the Strippit 750 is a desire to maintain that sense of control, to remain the master of "his" machine. And when he describes his many efforts to reach that end, it is not just "deskilling" he is talking about, but a kind of dispossession. "I feel degraded when they do this to me," says Boggs. "I've put in a lot. When you keep putting out and they're not picking up, you feel like it is all for nothing." The message he hears at work, he says, is "All we want you to do is come in here and push a button." It is a narrowing of his job, but a narrowing of his expectations as well. It destroys motivation, initiative, even pride. For Dave Boggs, the result is a "constant inner struggle" that mirrors the outer conflict over control. "Sometimes I feel like I should sue them for stealing my work." He pauses for a moment, then laughs lightly and adds, "Stealing my pride, I guess you could say."

Dave Boggs is a skilled worker, and it is perhaps the skilled craft-workers in the industrial sector who feel these contradictions of control most keenly. Because of their relatively high wages, they are a special target of the new technology. Because their jobs often involve some kind of maintenance of machines or production systems, they are the most affected by the move toward electronic technologies. Most important, because of their skills and their high degree of unionization, they exert a relatively broad range of control over their work. When that control is lost, they have the farthest to fall.

Few industries have experienced more technological change in recent years than telecommunications. Consider the example of what, until January 1, 1984, was America's largest private employer—the twenty-three operating companies and two major divisions of AT&T's Bell System. When AT&T introduced its first computer-controlled electronic switching system (ESS) in 1965, it was the beginning of a series of changes that would transform both telephone work and AT&T itself.

ESS is nothing less than a giant computer for electronically directing telephone signals from one phone to another. The most recent version to come from the scientists and engineers at Bell Labs is actually a whole network of computers—a labyrinthine web of microprocessors, light-guide fibers, and large-scale integrated circuits, woven together by over 200,000 separate software instructions.

With the spread of ESS throughout the central offices of the Bell System, some 140 other computer-based systems have grown up along with it. They monitor, administer, and maintain this vast computer web. They run on anywhere from 30,000 to 3 million lines of computer code. In the words of one Bell Labs engineer, "they keep our fingers to the pulse of the network." The computer has become so pervasive at the Bell operating companies that there is one video display terminal for every nine employees. And nearly half the technical workforce at Bell Labs now works producing the more than 18 million lines of computer code needed to fuel these systems—making Bell Labs one of the largest software houses in the world.

AT&T's Integrated Services Digital Network plan, introduced in 1981, gives an idea of where this massive computer network is heading. The corporation's ultimate goal is to convert the entire phone system from the traditional "continuous wave" signal (fine for transporting the human voice, but ill-suited for the rapid transmission of vast quantities of data) to the "on-off" digital code used in every computer. When that happens, the computerization of work in the American telecommunications system will be complete. Says Victor Vyssotsky, executive director of research at Bell Labs: "The whole telephone network will be one enormous computer."

But what do these changes mean for the central office technicians of the Bell System telecommunications network, who, across the country, are responsible for monitoring and maintaining this vast technological web? Traditionally, the telephone technician's job has involved not only a high degree of skill but also considerable autonomy. Electronic switching, however, has radically changed the work environment of the central office.

First, because of the transition from electromechanical to electronic switching, ESS cuts down on the need for switching technicians in some fairly simple and obvious ways. For example, the system is "self-diagnosing"; it monitors its own performance automatically by computer and figures out its own circuitry problems. Computers now do much of the analysis and "troubleshooting" that technicians used to do. Also, the new electronic systems have no moving parts, thus eliminating the need for mechanical repair skills. Technicians simply replace one malfunctioning circuit pack with another.

In addition, the computerization of the central office has made possible certain far-reaching organizational changes. Computer control of switching has allowed management to centralize the central office technicians' monitoring and repair functions. Automated Switching Control Centers now observe a number of central offices simultaneously by means of remote telemetry.

Computerization has also allowed the Bell operating companies to pursue their own version of computerized Taylorism, know as "functionalization." Whereas each switching technician in the central office used to be responsible for a range of diverse tasks, the concentration of work in the control center allows management to divide up these functions among the workforce. One traditional task, for example, was to identify and repair malfunctioning trunk lines. In the central office, a trunk-line "trouble report" would arrive on a teletype, and the technician would locate the trunk and put it out of service. Later, when he had the time to analyze the problem and devise a solution to it, he would return to repair the trunk. Now, trunk-line trouble reports from the central offices are all fed to the same control center, and all assigned to the same small group of technicians, who spend their entire day in front of VDT screens, keying messages to the computer to put the faulty trunks on "Busy." The technicians do not actually fix the malfunctioning lines themselves. This is a task for yet another group of "functionalized" specialists, organized into mobile units that travel from one central office to another to do the repairs on site. In the lingo of Bell switching technicians, they are known as "pack changers."

Perhaps the most dramatic changes in the way telephone workers do their jobs have been those affecting the "test-desk technician," the highest-paid skilled worker in the Bell System. Bill Tracy, who has worked as a tester at both New York Telephone in New York City and Southern Bell in Miami, Florida, thinks of his job as the "hub" of an intricate occupational wheel. In the traditional central office, the test-desk technician was the link between the office and telephone lines extending into businesses and homes. Whenever a customer reported malfunctioning equipment, it was his responsibility to locate the "trouble" in the maze of the telephone system, diagnose the problem, and dispatch repairmen or other personnel to fix it. In order to perform this job effectively, the tester had to know every facet of the various central office craft jobs and to coordinate the activities of many different departments. "The test-desk technician had to be well versed in all aspects of all the jobs," says Tracy, "whether he actually did them or not."

Beginning in 1976, AT&T introduced a computerized system designed to automate the tests performed by the test-desk technician. Known as mechanized loop testing or MLT, the system runs through a series of electronic tests on telephone lines at an extremely rapid pace. When a customer reports a problem, the operator of the MLT simply keys the number into the system and the computer performs its battery of tests. The system can also be programmed to go out looking for troubles by testing large blocks of numbers automatically. "The system monitors its own health," explains an engineer at Bell Labs. "That way, we know about a problem even before the customer does."

In the hands of an experienced test-desk technician, the MLT can be a formidable tool. Unfortunately, that is not exactly what AT&T had in mind. The primary purpose of this computerized maintenance system was not to enhance the tester's capabilities, but to cut labor costs. A memorandum from an AT&T vice-president to Bell System managers in Nashville (where MLT was first implemented) provides a flavor of prevailing corporate policy. "A word of caution," the executive warned. "The savings available from MLT implementation will only occur if you plan for them to occur and then actually get the people off the payroll. Too often, we are intrigued with the capabilities of new mechanized systems and forget the real reasons for their existence." In this case, the real reason was to get rid of the test-desk technician, and the MLT was assigned to lower-level clerks.

Bill Tracy was still working in New York City at the time of the introduction of MLT. His local union, the largest in the Communications Workers of America, which represents some 500,000 workers at AT&T and the Bell Operating Companies, disputed the company's MLT policy through the telephone industry's grievance procedure. The union argued that the computer is a tool just like any other. The MLT might be faster and, in certain cases, more efficient, but it is essentially no different from the meters on the test panel that the tester used in his work. Therefore, to assign to clerks a job traditionally performed by skilled craftsmen was to violate the integrity of the industry's negotiated occupational categories.

The arbitrator disagreed. Siding with the company, he found that computerization *transfers* skill from the worker to the machine. While the output of the two jobs was "generally similar," the arbitrator wrote, there was "no basic skill parity." In effect, the skills of the test-desk technician had been made obsolete. Moreover, the arbitrator argued that even if what the union claimed were true, the contract gave management an "absolute right" to assign work to whomever it chose. In its 1980 national contract, the CWA salvaged what it could. It negotiated a new occupational category, "maintenance administrators," to cover the new class of MLT operators. Their wage was set at 80 percent of the test-desk technician's pay, higher than any existing clerical category.

Testers have yet to be phased out entirely. The Bell System is letting "attrition" do its slow work. Some have been "surplused"—declared unnecessary and forced to retire or transfer to other offices or other regions of the country. Others have been kept on to handle the especially complicated troubles that are outside the MLT's electronic reach. At Southern Bell, however, where Bill Tracy moved from New York, the decline of the test-desk technician has taken another painful step. In August 1982, the company and District 3 of the Communications Workers union signed a supplemental agreement to the 1980 contract that effectively downgraded the remaining testers to the lower pay rate of the maintenance administrators. Bill Tracy and other testers learned of the decision just seven days before it was to go into effect. Starting September 1, 1982, Southern Bell testers began receiving $104 per week less in their telephone company paychecks.

But what is most revealing about the story of the test-desk technician is what has happened since. Despite this downgrading, getting the tester "off the payroll" may take longer than the engineers at Bell Labs first thought. In some Bell operating companies, the implementation of MLT has caused major problems. Far from eliminating the tester and reducing labor costs, it has, in certain cases, made testing circuits slower and more difficult than before.

The reasons why this is so are complex. Certainly few telephone workers would deny that technology like the MLT is of real value in the testing work process. Like Dave Boggs, they are fascinated with the new technology and understand its immense potential. The MLT performs certain tests faster than the test-desk technician could, it provides new kinds of information previously unavailable, and its ability to test entire blocks of circuits automatically contributes to preventive maintenance. But it is at the level of what one worker calls the "human, individual trouble" that the weaknesses of the system begin to show up. As a result, says Bob Krukles, president of CWA Local 3121, representing test-desk technicians and other telephone workers in Miami, "we're going crazy with the MLT test."

On the one hand, like many computer systems, the MLT is so fine-tuned and sensitive that it identifies "troubles" at the slightest provocation—and sometimes at no provocation at all. Krukles estimates that "trouble" reports have quadrupled in the Miami area since its installation. While some of these reports are certainly malfunctions that the test-desk technician missed, many involve only slight irregularities on the line that do not affect telephone service. Others are simply false. "We're seeing a lot of false trouble reports in the central offices," says Krukles.

While the hypersensitive MLT is identifying more troubles than ever before, it is also too unsophisticated to locate many of them precisely. "Things that the tester could find or determine," says Krukles, "the MLT can't." In the days when the test-desk technician was still the hub of the wheel, he was in close contact with the field personnel who were out tracking troubles down and repairing them. The two-way exchange between tester and repairman was an important element in resolving malfunctions quickly. With the new centralized system, this verbal contact has been replaced by a computer printout. The new maintenance administrators are rarely in touch with workers in the field. "They just give you the basics," explains Krukles, "and then you are on your own."

Derek Averett is one of the Southern Bell cable repairmen on the receiving end of the MLT reports. He is even less enthusiastic about the system than Krukles. "It's never right," says Averett. While the computer can identify what's wrong with a faulty telephone line, it has a hard time determining precisely where in the system the fault has occurred. As a result, workers in the field end up with less information than ever before. "You have to hit and miss," say Averett. "We rely on our old equipment—what the old test center used to have." In Miami, it takes longer to clear troubles now than ever before—Derek Averett estimates by about a third. In New York City, MLT has so extended the time it takes to clear malfunctions that New York Telephone has been forced to expand its testing workforce and put maintenance administrators and the few remaining testers on overtime. Telephone company managers have found that as much as they might like to, they can't entirely do away with the skilled test-desk technicians.

But the engineers of the Bell System have a solution to the shortcomings of MLT. A second generation of testing technology—dubbed MLT II—is now making its way into telephone offices. And an MLT III is already taking shape on the computerized design screens at Bell Labs. These ever more powerful, ever more versatile systems are supposed to resolve the recalcitrant difficulties of line testing work and do away with the test-desk technician once and for all.

Of course, in theory, there is nothing inherent in the new workplace technology that requires the kind of systematic deterioration of skills that telephone technicians have experienced. True, ESS has rendered electromechanical repair skills obsolete, but it requires new kinds of expertise in electronics-based systems and programming concepts. And, as the case of the test-desk technician suggests, the efficient use of computerized systems often requires workers with more skill than management thinks. Instead of downgrading workers, why not upgrade them, encourage their skills to evolve in tandem with technology itself?

From what many telephone workers say, they face a problem similar to that of Dave Boggs—but on a much larger scale. They have trouble acquiring the new skills necessary for the computerized workplace and even more difficulty using what new expertise they are able to obtain. Consider the example of the Electronics Systems Mini-Course. Established in 1982, its purpose was to ensure that Bell

System technicians had a rudimentary understanding of the principles of computer science. All technicians who wanted to be promoted to top craft categories had to pass the course. Some operating companies even made it a requirement for technicians already in those categories.

The term "course" is something of a misnomer. ESM was not a course but a test. The company claimed that it tested aptitude; it was the kind of test for which one could not prepare. What exactly the technicians were expected to know was never made entirely clear. "It's the biggest secret in the world," one CWA local union president told me, "like the combination to Fort Knox. They're not doing a thing to help people learn this stuff. They're doing testing, not training."

In an earlier, longer version of the test, failure rates in some areas of the country were as high as 85 percent. Even with the shortened mini-version, more than half the test-takers failed to pass. As the number of failed tests continued to pile up, telephone technicians began to see the "course" as part of a conscious company strategy to avoid the cost of training veteran workers for new computer-based jobs in favor of new employees, already trained. One calls the ESM test a "technological weeding out." Bob Krukles, in Miami, thinks it is a way for the company to "go to the street" without violating already-existing contractual provisions concerning seniority. A technician in San Francisco says, "It's very clear that the company is getting out of the education mode. They're more apt to hire people right out of college with high levels of training already."

Such comments may sound paranoid. And yet, with examples like that of the test-desk technician before their eyes, telephone workers are not taking any chances. Union locals have been setting up their own training programs to ensure that their members get through the ESM test. In Miami, Local 3121 has contracted with a professor of computer science at Florida International University to teach basic computer skills. In San Francisco, one local has a similar arrangement with a retired Bell System trainer. Five CWA locals in the Washington, D.C., area have established a Capitol Area Training Fund to help union members prepare for ESM and other company tests. As a result, telephone technicians have begun to pass the test regularly. Like Dave Boggs, they have become autodidacts of the brave new workplace.

Access to new skills is only one part of the retraining dilemma. Being able to use those skills, once acquired, is a crucial second step. In a workplace shaped by the assumptions of Taylorism, even the most elaborate training programs can lead to a frustrating dead end.

Joe Payne is a forty-five-year-old communications technician at AT&T Communications, the corporation's long-distance network, and a fifteen-year veteran of the company. In 1978, he attended a twenty-six-week comprehensive company training course to prepare him to work on the No. 4 ESS, at the time the most advanced electronic switching system in the Bell network. Payne was one of a group of about twelve technicians selected to implement the No. 4 at his Chester, Pennsylvania, central office.

The course Payne took was an exquisite model of intensive technological retraining. For half a year, he crisscrossed the country, acquiring an intimate familiarity with the new electronic switching system. In Baltimore, Payne learned his way through the forest of acronyms labeling the machine's myriad functions. In Atlanta, he studied the peripheral equipment linked to the main processor and picked up the basic ESS machine language. In Columbus, Ohio, he had a nine-day hands-on try-out with an already installed No. 4. Finally, like some high-technology circuit rider, Payne finished his tour in Chicago, where he devoted three and a half weeks to the machine's central processor. By the end of the training course, Payne had obtained a sound technological background in what he calls "the actual workings of the machine."

Ever since his training course, however, Payne has faced a central, and so far insurmountable, obstacle. "We got a lot of training that we have never been able to use," he says. At first, Payne chalked it up to the fabled efficiency of electronic switching. "The programming in the machine is so good," he says. "It has its own maintenance program. There are so few really detailed troubles. And there are so many software changes coming down that the machine keeps getting better and better." Yet the deeper reason why his new technological skills have remained stillborn is that AT&T managers have chosen to organize the communications technicians' work so that he cannot use them.

According to the planners of the brave new workplace, the virtuosity of the ESS machine should not keep Joe Payne from exercising his new skills. While certain tasks become easier (and others disappear altogether) because of computerization, this only serves to free Payne up to work on more interesting and more complex "systems" troubles. Yet, not long after the new No. 4 ESS equipment was installed in the Philadelphia area, the company also established a Systems Maintenance Control Center (SMCC) in Washington, D.C., with access to all the ESS machines in a multistate area. It receives the same trouble reports that the local offices receive. The purpose of SMCC is to monitor not one machine, but the entire network. And while some of the workers who were in Payne's training course were promoted to the SMCC office, not all could be. It is staffed entirely by management personnel.

Ever since the creation of the SMCC office, the responsibilities of Joe Payne's job have been steadily chipped away. First the regular announcements of changes in ESS software stopped coming into the local office; they were routed directly to the SMCC instead. Then the maintenance center announced a work standard requiring local offices to solve any local troubles within two hours. As soon as the time limit elapsed, the unsolved problem would be taken over by the management experts in Washington. Over a period of time, the SMCC gained more and more of the crucial "on-the-job" experience in solving the more complicated system problems and Joe Payne got less and less. Eventually, he and other technicians in the field stopped receiving basic information about ESS operations.

"It became very frustrating," says Payne. "We felt we had got all this schooling and it's useless." Sitting in the electronic shadow of SMCC, Payne's job became that of a high-tech machine tender. The ESS computer would keep spitting out the identical trouble report. Payne and his co-workers would work feverishly to get it fixed within the two-hour limit. "You didn't have any idea what was causing it," he remembers. "You didn't know what to do. You'd just keep trying to fix it." Then, after two hours of failure, when they would reluctantly contact the Washington maintenance center, they would be told, "Oh, yeah, we know about that. It's a change in the software. Don't worry about it." It was, says Payne, "a brush-off answer—because you're not the expert anymore."

It would be absolutely wrong to say that Joe Payne's skills have been made "obsolete" by new technology. As he says, "I've learned a lot about computer skills." Nevertheless, the very structure of his job has kept him from using them. In a sense, his job has been split in two. The most interesting "system skills" have disappeared into management, and only those tasks shorn of skill have been left behind.

"You are no longer offered anything," says Payne. "They used your help to install the system, took the top two or three people down to the SMCC, and took away our jobs by remoting them." Payne has since transferred out of the ESS office, but he keeps in touch with his former colleagues. "Now, it's worse there than ever. The guys sit around. They're more clerks than they are technicians. When it comes to the real troubles, they just have to go somewhere else for support. They're not really doing anything that they went to school for."

Payne's story suggests a pattern common to technological change and training in the brave new workplace. The time when new technological systems require a broadly skilled workforce is at the very beginning, when they are being installed. But once systems are functioning smoothly, the need for skills diminishes. Workers in the right place at the right time may acquire new skills and even get better jobs. Others, like Payne, learn the skills but never really use them. And those who follow may never obtain the same degree of training and expertise as their predecessors.

Since Joe Payne went to ESS school, the technician's training course has been substantially scaled back. Payne says that it usually amounts to five or six weeks, the minimum necessary for a technician to "be functional." At the most, communications technicians might eventually receive eighteen weeks of training on ESS, still far less than Payne's twenty-six weeks. What is perhaps the typical management attitude toward training was expressed by a Bell Labs technician running a demonstration of SARTS, a special-circuits-testing system similar to the MLT. Asked how long it took to learn how to operate the system, he replied that people "learn by doing" in a course that lasts two weeks. "They bring in people with no computer experience," he said. "They tend to be folks who have just been hired." Working on SARTS, he continued, "requires no knowledge of the computer. A naive person who doesn't know much about computers or testing is probably better at SARTS than some experienced tester who thinks he knows what testing is. I don't think there is any particular expertise necessary."

Attitudes such as these have created insecurity and even fear among workers like Joe Payne. "Guys are worried because they see their jobs going," says Payne. "They look at the No. 4 ESS offices and they see it starts out with a lot of workers. The attitude used to be, 'Great, let's get the No. 4. We'll learn the new technology and we'll be all set.' Now they see that after the new technology is in for a couple of years, they're forcing guys out because they don't need them anymore. There's no security, not even in being involved in the new technology."

Joe Payne uses a metaphor that one hears from many telephone technicians. He says that his job is being reduced to that of a "clerk." From the perspective of clerical workers themselves, however, one might expect a radically different attitude about the computerization of work. After all, it is precisely these low-level, dead-end jobs—looked upon with such dismay by craftworkers—that have the most to gain from a reorganization of work accompanying the new technology. And for the women who, by a large majority, occupy them, technology holds the potential for getting rid of onerous tasks and opening up new possibilities for advancement. Better to have computerized customer records at your fingertips rather than buried in mammoth files. Better to edit a letter on the screen of a word processor than to type and retype draft after draft. And whatever the test-desk technicians may think of the new maintenance administrators, no one can deny that for the clerical workers—again, mostly women—who have moved into these new jobs, they represent an important step up.

And yet the impact of computerization on clerical work is rarely so simple. Where technology is used as an instrument of control, it can make clerical jobs as rigid and as onerous as ever. In fact, many technology managers are prisoners of an outdated and inaccurate conception of clerical work. In the office, their romance with Taylorism can have particularly disastrous results.

I first realized this on a visit to a brand-new Automated Repair Service Bureau at Michigan Bell in Detroit, Michigan. About fifty women sat in a cavernous room, separated into groups of four, their eyes glued to the cathode flicker of jet-black video display terminals. They fielded call after call, quickly typing the information provided by customers into the computer, then passing it along to the appropriate repair units with a push of a button. At the front of the room, a screen displayed the office's "speed of answer" by means of a color graph. Noticing my presence, a manager—male—came rushing over to explain how the office operated. "These girls," he said, "are just an interface between the customer and the computer."

Diana Osborne first learned about the gap between the promise of information technology and the managerial assumptions that see workers as an "interface" when eight VDTs suddenly appeared in her circuit design office at Southwestern Bell in Houston, Texas. At first, "nobody really understood what it was about," remembers Osborne. "It wasn't really taken seriously at all." Gradually, however, as office workers slowly began to find their way through the new computer system, they discovered that it gave them access to all kinds of information, that it was a window into a world of new skills and new opportunities. "We began to understand that there was all kinds of information in it," says Osborne. "I could learn things that even some of the engineers didn't know." For example, one day Osborne discovered by chance that the computer system included a learning program by the name of Tutor. When you entered the proper password, the message "Hello, I am Tutor" would flash on the screen, followed by lessons in the use of the system.

There was only one problem. The responsibilities of Osborne's job were so narrow and her workload so heavy that she didn't have the time to explore the new skills that computerization had potentially made available. Even worse, her supervisor discouraged the clerks from using the Tutor program, even to the point of trying to keep secret the password for accessing it. "They don't want you to know how to get into Tutor," says Osborne. "You could learn anything—the sky is the limit—if only they'd let you. But you have to push them."

The major obstacle to learning new skills at the Houston circuit design office was the high work quotas and the computerized system for monitoring worker performance that accompanied the automation of the office. Osborne would receive a computer printout listing her output for the day. Once the new system was implemented, clerks were expected to complete thirty-six special circuits each day—more than anyone had ever done before. And while the printout listed each worker's tally, it neglected to indicate how often and for how long the computer itself was down—a common occurrence, especially in the first months of the new system.

At weekly productivity meetings with her boss, Osborne and other clerical workers in the Houston office reviewed their work performance. "I kept telling them it wasn't a fair quota," says Osborne. She was told there was nothing to be done; the standards had been set at Southwestern Bell headquarters in St. Louis. Other offices had it even worse. In one word-processing department, consisting of some thirty clerks, only two had made the official keystroke quota. Their supervisor gave the entire office an unsatisfactory rating.

Osborne and her colleagues eventually resorted to a slowdown in their efforts to get the quota changed. What they achieved was an uneasy compromise. Management never officially revoked the quota. Supervisors simply agreed not to discipline those workers who failed to meet it. This wasn't enough, however, to keep Osborne's flicker of interest in her job—sparked by the new technology—alive. By the end of her stay in the special circuits office, her excitement had been replaced by an all too familiar anomie. "You just type on your machine all day," she remembers. "You're tied to your desk a lot more." And for every circuit that a clerk completes on her VDT, she types in her initials so the computerized monitoring system can keep an accurate track of her work performance.

Her managers did not allow Diana Osborne the increased responsibility that the new technology made possible in her office. But even in "responsible" jobs, using technology as an instrument of control can undermine whatever sense of satisfaction or accomplishment moving up the job ladder can engender among clerical workers. Consider the example of Ann Princiotta, a service representative at New Jersey Bell. The job of the service representative is extremely important, since the rep is the customer's first contact with the company. She is responsible not only for taking orders, but for informing customers of new products and trying to persuade them to buy services or products they did not have in mind or perhaps did not know about.

And yet, Princiotta's work is rigidly structured by the measurement and scheduling of the office computer. Both the time she takes with customer orders over the telephone and the "down time" during which she follows up on customer requests, does her paperwork, and generally catches up are scheduled in fifteen-minute segments. The computer tells the office supervisor how many reps to have answering the phones for every fifteen-minute segment of the day (based on a complicated statistical survey of previous calls to that office in the past). If a customer request is the least bit complicated, so as to require further checking, the rep must wait for her assigned down time. What's more, "you're not supposed to tell the customer, 'Sorry, but I can't handle this until this afternoon,' " says Princiotta. "You're supposed to say, 'I'll check into it and call you by five.' " Even worse, if during any quarter-hour fewer reps are available to handle calls than mandated by the computer, a rep's down time can be taken away. "You're told by the supervisor, 'You have to be available because our bodies don't meet the quota the machine is calling for.' " And whenever the rep puts a customer on hold—in order to check a price or verify the first available delivery date—she is timed to see how long she keeps the customer waiting. "You are always under the time clock," says Princiotta. "It's always running and you know somebody is timing you."

Ann Princiotta certainly has responsibilities in her service rep job. The problem is, she doesn't have the authority to shape her workday in the way she thinks best. "You're not in control of being able to help the customer when he wants it," she says. "You don't have the authority to take care of the customer the way you think you should." And when workers lose control, quality suffers.

What explains the difficulties that the computerization of work poses for clerical workers like Diana Osborne and Ann Princiotta, difficulties that affect not only the quality of their work experience but that of the very services they provide? Part of the explanation is that built into management's assumptions about Taylorism is an inadequate conception of what most office workers really do.

This misunderstanding is made clear in some recent research on office work and office automation coming out of Xerox's Palo Alto Research Center in Silicon Valley, based on detailed ethnographic studies of how office workers actually do their jobs. It challenges some of our most common assumptions about clerical work. While many people—and most technology managers—see office work as routine and "mindless," Xerox researchers have uncovered the hidden dimension to clerical work and the truth that successful performance of office procedures is fundamentally an "intellectual" process.

Put simply, the routine procedure that, for most of us, "defines" office work is merely an idealized representation of what a clerk actually does. The clear-cut functions and workplace routines spelled out in job descriptions and management manuals are "ideal types"—expressions of the final goals of office work rather than descriptions of the work itself. Behind these precise routines and procedures, a vast realm of informal and unstructured activities are in fact essential to "realizing" these office functions. They are invisible to the outsider and, to the degree that they are part of the occupational common sense of a particular office, they are invisible to workers as well. In the language of the Xerox researchers, these informal and largely invisible practices make up the world of "practical action."

These informal practices and techniques are not spelled out in job manuals and training materials. Rather, they are part of the "latent information" of any clerical workplace. They constitute the necessary information, interpretations, precedents, and gloss that allow the application of the explicit procedures in any specific case. Office work is intellectual work in the sense that it is a continuous exercise in problem-solving—searching out and creating information in order to bring the general rules and procedures to bear in each particular set of circumstances.

Take, for example, the job of a credit representative responsible for collecting overdue bills.* The job, of course, is actually to collect the money owed on those bills. But in the course of accomplishing that "routine" procedure, she may be led to solve any number of problems in an informal way. She might have to convince a particular customer, who disputes the sum, that the specified amount is indeed owed. She might have to understand what it takes for the customer's organization actually to issue a check and negotiate the time it will take. She might have to devise a strategy to get her counterparts in the customer's organization "on her side" to facilitate the check-issuing process and informally negotiate with any number of people—in both the customer's organization and her own—to keep the payment process moving along. And sometimes she might even have to know how to short-circuit the "official" procedure in order to clear the way for a quick payment. Such activities extend far beyond the instructions that any clear-cut procedures provide. They are part of the social lore of the workplace, embedded in the very social fabric of office life.

In this respect, office work as "problem-solving" is a profoundly social activity. The development of latent information takes place through conversations and inquiries—with co-workers, with other departments in the organization, with managers, with customers. And the act of work itself is an elaborate series of social exchanges through which information is acquired, verified, interpreted, and applied to formal procedures and routines.

This understanding of office work has enormous implications for office automation. Most technology managers, armed with the principles of Taylorism, concentrate on the formal procedures of office work and see the realm of informal practical action as a "problem," part of the stubborn ambiguity of clerical work, to be

---

* This example is drawn from "Procedures and Problems in the Office Environment," by Lucy Suchman and Eleanor Wynn, Xerox Advanced Systems Department, April 1979.

"rationalized," eliminated, or, when it cannot, ignored. Often the final result is to create rigid technological systems that violate the very logic of the work they are supposed to automate.

The Automated Repair Service Bureaus of the Bell System provide a simple example. Workers there use a system known as the Line Maintenance Operating System (LMOS), which is basically a computerized file. When a repair service attendant takes a call from a customer reporting malfunctioning equipment, she types the customer's telephone number into the computer and receives a complete record of past problems on her VDT screen. The clerk adds the information provided by the customer and gives a "commitment time" (provided by the computer) indicating when a repair crew will visit the customer's home. Then she transfers the record, trouble report, and commitment time to the repair garage via computer.

LMOS sounds wonderfully efficient, a logical progression of clear-cut work steps. But according to repair service clerks, it isn't. "It's easier in getting information," says one repair service attendant, "but as far as getting your phone fixed, it takes a lot longer now than it ever did before." The problem, of course, is that things don't always work out so smoothly as the LMOS program suggests. Any number of spontaneous problems can develop along the way—for example, last-minute changes in the repair truck's schedule, a backup in repair work, a customer suddenly changing his commitment time.

Before LMOS, repair service attendants worked in local repair bureaus, organizationally attached to the central offices. They were in frequent telephone contact with repair and installation crews. Often they would relay messages between customers and crews, informing them of changes in plans. "You knew how many men you had on the street," says the repair service attendant, "how many troubles you could handle." With LMOS, all the attendants now work in centralized automated bureaus. Their only contact with the crews is one-way, via the computer. They do not know if the crew actually makes it to the customer's house at the appointed time (although, often, they have to listen to the customer's complaints when it does not). "Now, you're doing it blindly," says the clerk. "You're not able to give it the little personal touch you did before."

If the insights of Xerox researchers are accurate, this "personal touch" is no dispensable luxury. It is a social activity essential to the effective performance of clerical work. LMOS has destroyed the informal network of communication and problem-solving that made the repair procedures function. The result is a rigid computerized work system that not only shackles workers to narrow and inflexible jobs ("just an interface between the customer and the computer") but disrupts the effective performance of the work itself.

Why not install LMOS directly into the local repair centers? That way, clerks would have the convenience and efficiency of computerization with the flexibility and informal communication of the local work unit. But this would require changing some of the fundamental assumptions by which new technology is designed—in particular, abandoning the presumption that the purpose of new technology is to expand managerial control.

The most disturbing example of technology used as an instrument of control is the practice of computerized productivity monitoring described by Steve Taylor and the vice-president at Citicorp in Chapter 1. While nobody knows for sure precisely how many workers are subject to monitoring, there is evidence to suggest that it is a daily fact of life for many people in the brave new workplace. A recent nationwide survey of video display terminal operators, conducted by 9 to 5, the National Association of Working Women, revealed that some 35 percent were monitored by computer. Word-processing clerks, insurance claims processors, customer service representatives, postal workers, data entry workers, bank tellers, supermarket cashiers, waiters and waitresses, hotel maids, even truck drivers have all seen such systems introduced to their workplaces. But few workers are more subject to the rigid control of computerized monitoring than those at the low end of the occupational hierarchy in the telecommunications industry—telephone operators.

In a typical operators' office, workers sit in long rows, plugged into the battleship-gray terminals of the Traffic Service Position System, or TSPS. Calls "drop in" to the console with an electronic beep. Fingers flash over a bewildering array of buttons. In a matter of seconds, the call is completed, only to be followed by another beep and another call. The office's Automatic Call Distributor routes a new call to each TSPS position the instant a line is free. The usual gap between calls is usually only a matter of seconds. The office's Call Waiting Box indicates any calls into the office not yet dispatched to a single terminal. If a call remains waiting beyond a ten-second limit, a light begins to flash. This is called a "late answer." The Call Waiting Box also signals whenever any of the terminals in the office have been disconnected or put on busy.

For up to two and a half hours at any one time, operators field call after call without a break. "You'd think you were at the Indianapolis Speedway," says one. "If you don't keep your AWT down, they start riding you." AWT stands for "average working time" per call. The norm in most offices is usually about thirty seconds. When the office AWT creeps over this standard or when the blinking lights of the Call Waiting Board flash on, supervisors fan out among the long rows of operators in a well-choreographed effort to speed up the pace. Operators hurry to disconnect, often so fast that their ritual "Have a happy day" is clipped in midsentence. A supervisor at one TSPS office admits that the job can get rough sometimes. "But it can also be very rewarding," she adds, "especially if you like to talk with people."

Every fifteen minutes of the day, in Bell operator offices across the country, computer terminals near supervisors' desks print out the office's complete productivity record. In a ragged, staccato tempo, these Quarter-Hour Summaries list how many operators were on duty, how many calls they handled, the average working time per call, the number of late answers, even the average "speed of answer"—how long before an operator responds to the electronic beep signaling yet another incoming call. To get the productivity record of an individual employee is almost as easy. A supervisor merely keys the employee's number into the computer, and within seconds it prints out her performance for the day. In some offices, these daily records are kept in a black book prominently displayed on a stand near the door to the office, accessible to supervisors and operators alike.

The Quarter-Hour Summary is a product of AT&T's computerized Force Administration System, or FADS. Every fifteen minutes, as the FADS computers start compiling their update, supervisors scramble as if on cue to fill out a form listing the number of operators on duty and whether it was over or under the computerized projection of workforce needs made by FADS. Since the system automatically schedules workers for fifteen-minute intervals, supervisors also know immediately whether anyone is late for work or returning from lunch or break. Latenesses and absences are duly recorded, and all the information is sent to the Centralized Administration Group, or CAG, the brain of every TSPS office. There it is tabulated and added to the ongoing record of office performance, a record that never stops accumulating—every fifteen minutes, twenty-four hours a day.

Such intricate computerized monitoring of work takes the technology managers' vision of control to its logical, extreme conclusion. When managers talk about monitoring, they tend to dismiss the idea that it might have negative effects on workers' sense of themselves and their work. Judith Reitman at Bell Labs admits that the computer systems of the operator office provide "an overwhelming amount of data" to office managers. But she is not especially concerned about the effect of this constant workplace monitoring. "Some people like to challenge themselves," she says. "It's like timing yourself around the track. Operators have been tracked for many years. They're paid to do things quickly and correctly; they're paid for average work time. That is going to shape their behavior immensely. Whatever performance standards they are given, they will adapt."

The manager at Citicorp admits that his MIS Daily Operating Report gives managers "more control over the system." But he justifies this control by claiming that the information provided by the report is not used against people in any systematic way. "To what extent you use that control is up to you," he says reassuringly. "We haven't quite taken it to the level that a good management consultant would want us to." Nevertheless, should someone—the Citicorp clerk in Chicago perhaps—not be performing up to par, "you have the ability to go after him, right down to every minute of the workday." Eventually he admits, "we've done it many times." With MIS, "we take the excuses away."

Whether such computerized monitoring systems are used to discipline particular individuals is, finally, beside the point. It is enough that they exist, a kind of software sword of Damocles suspended over people's heads, ready to be brought into play at management's discretion. Worse, this fundamental arbitrariness is disguised by the seeming objectivity of the data. To the degree that the unambiguous measurements of the computer are "scientific," they have the appearance of rationality. They serve to obscure the very relationship of unequal power that they reinforce. "It's a very rigid control," says one Citibank systems designer. "In the past, we've always had supervision that was irregular. Now, the control is no longer personal. After all, computers don't like or dislike people." In a sense, control becomes "automatic," just like work itself. And the reality of power disappears behind the impersonality of the machine.

The language of workers reflects this change. "We don't work for the supervisor anymore," says Derek Averett in Miami, "we're working for the computers now."

"That machine is telling you what to do," says Bob Krukles. "It's controlling your daily activities. The computer now tells you what your productivity is. That machine is telling you when you're doing good and when you're doing bad."

"The computer watches you for the supervisor," says a service representative in Washington, D.C. "It is constantly alert to the atmosphere of the office. If you close your terminal, right away the computer starts clacking away and starts ringing a bell."

A repair service attendant in New York City describes her newly computerized job as "being on the hot seat."

But, of course, this impersonality of control is a chimera, and the appearance of rationality is a myth. Monitoring often does not even serve the narrowest ends of economic efficiency that are its ostensible justification. One Citibank supervisor, for example, tells the story of a two-minute "average working time" placed on all calls to customer representatives at the bank's bank-card processing center in South Dakota. What happened was that as workers anxiously approached the end of the time limit on each call, they would hang up on their customers whether the conversation was completed or not. Another manager at the bank complains that automated control systems measure quantity but not quality, what he terms the "degree of difficulty" of different tasks. "It just spits out data," he says. "It only tells you how many items you've resolved."

Yet, no matter what misgivings about monitoring individual managers might have, the temptation—and the pressure—to rely on such quantitative data is enormous and virtually irresistible. The numbers of the computer seem so concrete, so unequivocal and "hard." They are the embodiment of the technology managers' ideal of perfection. "Sometimes," says the Citibank manager who worries about the degree of difficulty, "the risk of technology is that you become a slave of the system. If I see a bad printout and don't know the person involved, it makes me say, 'This guy with an 87 didn't do his job.' " Indeed, the system even becomes a means to judge the performance not only of workers but of first-line managers. "The job of the manager is to make sure that worker performance stays high," says the vice-president at Citicorp, "so this is a tool to measure the manager as well."

Finally, in many cases, the impetus for such intricate tracking of work comes from above—from the Citicorp managers in New York, perusing the daily operating report of some clerk in Chicago; from the Southwestern Bell systems designers in St. Louis, setting the quota for Diana Osborne's office in Houston; from the Bell Labs engineers in New Jersey and Illinois, creating the narrow work systems for telephone operators across the country. Thus, the computerization of work contributes to what technology consultant Peter Keen has called the "effective recentralization of management."

What is true for computerized monitoring is true for the Taylorist use of new technology as a whole. It too has the appearance of rationality. It too is justified by traditional economic values of efficiency and productivity. It too is a kind of myth in which the realities of corporate power disappear behind the opaque impersonality of the machine.

Of all the managers to whom I spoke while exploring the changes taking place at work, none saw the implications of a workplace where "the system must be first" more clearly than Steve Taylor himself. Talking about his experiences at Texas International, Taylor imagines what it would be like "being one of those persons who sits down at a terminal and keystrokes all day." He would put in his eight hours and go home, thinking he "had done a pretty good job," only to have his supervisor come up to him the next morning, printout in hand, and say: "Well, Steve, it looks like you had an off day yesterday; what's the problem?" Sometimes, Taylor thinks, it is more trouble than it's worth. "Whenever you start reducing the span of control like that, whenever you reduce things to numbers, to me, that increases the alienation and the pressure. The pressure of the computer."

Of course, Taylor also subscribes to the myth. For it is not the computer that is the ultimate source of the pressure he describes. Rather, it is the social choice to use new technology in order to expand the corporation's control over work.

CHAPTER THREE

PERSONAL
COSTS

THIRTY HOURS EVERY WEEK, a woman I shall call Elaine Jensen sits before her video display terminal in a small data-entry shop on the South Side of Chicago, keying information from insurance premium forms into a computer. The forms, from independent insurance agents around the country, are shipped to the Chicago office of a major national accounting firm, then sent down from the Loop to Jensen's workplace on the South Side, where some forty women on three shifts turn the data on the forms into magnetic messages on computer tape.

Jensen's job is at the bottom of the occupational hierarchy of the brave new workplace. In a normal six-hour day, she processes anywhere from 2,700 to 3,200 forms—roughly eight every minute. She thinks of her work as "the equivalent of a factory-type job, putting on bolts all day," although she admits that "usually, they get paid a lot more than we do." Jensen currently makes $5 an hour (before a recent raise, her wage was $3.75). She has no official breaks during her workday; she receives neither paid vacation nor pension. However, she can put in her thirty hours at any time of the day or night, an important advantage for a mother with two young children. (In 1982, 18.3 million Americans, nearly one-fifth of the total employed workforce and one-third of employed women, worked part-time. While overall employment was growing by 26.5 percent between 1970 and 1982, part-time employment was rising by 57.9 percent.)

The bad pay, poor working conditions, and boring work are not the worst aspects of Elaine Jensen's job. What she hates most of all is the unremitting pressure of data-entry work. It's not just the mind-deadening routine or the constant pressure for production. (At one point, she says, "In any other office, people stop and chat; in data entry, they just expect you to plug away without a moment's break.") It's not even the fact that her VDT can compile up-to-the-minute data on her performance, available to her supervisor at the push of a button. What irks Jensen the most is that she can never fade out. However boring it may be, her job requires that she maintain her concentration, pay attention to her forms and her typing in order to keep up the pace and avoid mistakes. The pressure of her job comes from the simple fact that "you have to concentrate on what you're doing."

As a result, says Jensen, every day is a constant struggle to "keep our minds on our work." She and the other workers at the South Side data-entry shop are caught in a peculiar double bind. On the one hand, their work is so boring, the pace so intense, that the natural tendency is to block it out. The feeling is a little like what happens when you are driving on a long, grueling automobile trip and "all of a sudden, you don't know how you got from one place to another." And yet, when this happens, Jensen's speed declines and her accuracy deteriorates, and she begins to feel guilty about not doing a good job. "Maybe it's just me," she says, "but when I know the work is there waiting, I just want to get it out."

So, Jensen's work becomes a battle against the kind of detachment that, for all its disadvantages, is at least one solution to the unpleasantness of a routine job. She has tried any number of tricks to overcome her sense of disengagement at work. For a time, she listened to the radio, but finally she found it too distracting. Now, when she feels the pressure and anxiety build, she has gotten into the habit of getting up from her desk, walking around, perhaps getting something to eat from the vending machines in the back of the office (she has gained twenty pounds in the five years she has worked at the data-entry shop). The breaks are a relief, but the forms next to her desk pile up, and soon she is drawn back to the peremptory glow of her VDT.

Jensen's most successful technique for keeping her mind on her work involves an account that passes her way every now and then—insurance premiums for expensive antique cars. Some of the cars are owned by well-known celebrities, and Jensen likes to prime herself for the moment when she can type one of their names onto her screen. She ticks off some of her "clients" in a voice tinged with an ironic occupational pride. "Let's see," she says, "I've had Neil Sadeka, Barbra Streisand, Steve McQueen's kids." It is something to look forward to, a moment of engagement, a glimmer of variety in an otherwise undifferentiated and monotonous day.

From the 20th of each month to the 10th of the next, Elaine Jensen and the other data-entry workers face a period known as "closing," during which they must complete all the accounts they have been working on for the previous month. During closing, the normal pressures of the data-entry job intensify to the breaking point. At the height of the last closing, Elaine Jensen was processing over 4,800 forms in her six-hour day—about thirteen every minute. Her eyes became blurry and began to burn (since she began working with a video display terminal ten months before, she has had to get glasses for the first time in her life). Sitting at the screen for hours at a stretch, her shoulders and back began to ache; the circulation was cut off to her legs and her lower body felt numb. As each day brought the final deadline of closing nearer, Jensen felt an overwhelming fatigue. And yet, at the same time, she became more and more anxious. The pile of forms at the side of her desk was a constant reproach; her stomach would tighten at the sight of them, as she would hurriedly try to calculate how much longer they would take, then plunge back into her work with renewed urgency.

In a flurry of frantic activity, Jensen finally met her deadline. But she went home at the end of the last day of closing totally exhausted. She couldn't make dinner; the thought of watching television made her slightly sick; she even found it impossible to sit down. Instead, she sprawled on her living-room floor and put her feet up on a pile of cushions. As if on signal, like a spring wound too tight, then suddenly released, Elaine Jensen's body began to tremble uncontrollably. And the tension and pressure of the previous three weeks revisited her on her living-room floor.

People experience their lack of control in the brave new workplace in many different ways. For Dave Boggs, it is the disappearance of the skills and the sense of mastery he once knew. For Diana Osborne, it is the inability to take advantage of the new opportunities that technology should make possible but that her supervisor denies her. For Ann Princiotta, it is the contradiction between the responsibilities of her service-rep job and the lack of authority to meet those responsiblities as she thinks best. For Elaine Jensen, however, this pervasive absence of control goes even farther, touching her sense of physical and psychological well-being. For her, the brave new workplace has become a source of occupational stress.

Stress is an experience that most of us have had at one time or another—and perhaps nowhere more commonly than at work. The iron pressure of a deadline; the frantic juggling of too many tasks and responsibilities; that clutching feeling in the chest when things get to be too much. Aren't we all, in some sense, victims of occupational stress? Fortunately, the answer is no—because whatever the pressures we may feel in our jobs, usually they are temporary. The deadline comes and goes; the tasks get done, the responsibilities are met. Most of us have the possibility—call it the institutional and organizational space—to cope with these pressures and overcome them. And then, our work returns to normal, at least until the demands pile up once again.

But what happens when, as in the case of Elaine Jensen, stress becomes not occasional but chronic? What happens when it is with us every single minute of the day? When stress becomes constant, it ceases to be merely some unpleasant but temporary challenge. Strictly speaking, it becomes an occupational health hazard as dangerous as any toxic chemical or unsafe machine. And it can cause physical sickness such as headaches, insomnia, fatigue, and, over the long term, hypertension and coronary heart disease; or psychological sickness like anxiety, depression, and, in extreme cases, even a nervous breakdown.

The very term "stress" has only recently become part of accepted medical terminology. The reason is that it does not fit in easily to the traditional medical model of what constitutes a disease. Most diseases can be traced to specific physiological causes; they have a clear-cut explanatory framework or "etiology." But stress involves a complicated interaction between the environment and the individual which makes causality in any specific instance extremely difficult to determine. In certain cases, a variety of different environmental factors can lead to the identical stress-related symptom. In others, the same factor will produce a variety of symptoms in different individuals.

In part because of this uncertainty about the causes of stress, we tend to make a common mistake when we think about it. We focus on only one side of the story. Either particular individuals seem especially prone to stress; it is a "personal" problem. Or stress seems to be, somehow, everywhere—an inevitable given of "modern society." Some of the most interesting recent research on stress, however, takes a more discriminating approach. It sees the causes of stress as "psychosocial." This perspective matches the occurrence of stress-related symptoms in specific human populations with the characteristics of particular social environments. And one environment where the occurrence of stress is being closely studied is the workplace.

That work can have an extensive psychological impact on the individual has been a truism of industrial sociology at least since the early 1950s. In 1952, Charles Walker and Robert Guest published a pioneering study of an American automobile plant entitled *Man on the Assembly Line,* a compelling portrait of how the mechanical work pace and the rigidly fragmented tasks of the Taylorist factory were major causes of job dissatisfaction and psychological stress for those who worked there. Over the next twenty-five years, researcher after researcher emphasized the role of mass-production technology and the pacing of work by machine as a central cause of stress on the job.

A central assumption of much of this research was that as technology advanced, it would eliminate many of the most stressful aspects of assembly-line work. Perhaps the most famous example of this perspective was Robert Blauner's *Alienation and Freedom,* first published in 1964. Blauner compared the attitudes of workers about their jobs in three quite different workplaces—a small artisanal printing shop, a mass-production assembly line, and a highly automated continuous-process oil refinery. What he found was that people's feelings about their jobs corresponded to a U-shaped curve. The high job satisfaction of the printers disappeared by the time one got to the line workers of the mass-production factory, only to reappear again in the technical workers of the automated refinery. And the reason was that the workers in the highly technical work environment of the refinery enjoyed the same kind of discretion and control over their work as did the workers in the craft setting—albeit at a much higher level of technological sophistication. Blauner's conclusion was that technology would liberate the worker from the stresses of the assembly line.

Recent research, however, has begun to challenge this faith in the soothing effects of technology. For it recognizes the simple fact that the most modern of technologies can be joined to the most traditional and authoritarian of work organizations. And when this happens, the result is often not less occupational stress, but more.

Consider, for example, the body of empirical research completed during the past ten years on the potential health effects of that most ubiquitous building block of the computerized workplace, the video display terminal. Numerous field studies in both the United States and Europe have shown that VDT operators report the same kind of health complaints as those Elaine Jensen describes. Physical symptoms commonly include blurred vision, irritated eyes, and other signs of ocular discomfort; chronic pains in the back, neck, and shoulders; and frequent headaches. The more time spent working at the terminals, the greater the frequency of complaints. At the same time, reports of psychological indications of stress—insomnia, feelings of fatigue, nervousness, and depression—have also been unusually common among VDT workers. In their first comprehensive study of the health effects of VDTs, researchers at the federal government's National Institute of Occupational Safety and Health (NIOSH) found that clerical workers who used video display terminals full-time exhibited the highest levels of stress ever reported in a NIOSH survey—even higher than those of air-traffic controllers.

What has caused this rash of health complaints? It seems clear that a great many of the symptoms, especially the physical ones, are the direct result of the poor design of the new technology itself. A terminal with blurred characters or a screen with a frequent flicker can seriously strain the human eye. So can poor lighting or screen glare. A keyboard that does not detach from the screen, a screen that does not tilt to allow workers to adjust it for the most comfortable viewing angle, or even a chair that is too low or too high can contribute to chronic pains in the back, neck, and shoulders. Thus the simplest solution to some of the health problems associated with the new technology is "ergonomics"—the design of technology so that it conforms to the physiology of the human body, rather than forcing the body to conform to it.

Health problems can also be caused by continuous work on VDTs. NIOSH has recommended that VDT operators be given a fifteen-minute "work-rest break" after every two hours of nonstop VDT use, or after every hour when that work is especially heavy. Regular rest breaks would go even further than the ergonomic design of display terminals toward eliminating stress for VDT workers.

But when it comes to the more complicated and less visible psychological symptoms of occupational stress, focusing on the technology does not go anywhere near far enough. For it may well be that the ultimate cause is not so much the shape of the machine or even the amount of time that an individual works on it as the shape of the job itself—and workers' ability to control what they are doing.

A closer look at the NIOSH VDT study demonstrates this vividly. In late 1979, NIOSH researchers administered a health survey to workers at five workplaces in the San Francisco Bay Area. The respondents were divided into three categories: professional journalists at three Bay Area newspapers who used VDTs for writing and editing; clerical workers at the Oakland office of Blue Shield who used the terminals all day either to enter data into a computerized filing system or for word processing; and a control group of non-VDT users working in the same Blue Shield office.

The journalists were primarily reporters and editors who worked at their terminals only sporadically and whose jobs, according to the NIOSH report, "afforded a great deal of self-control over work activities which provided variety and challenge." The clerical VDT operators, on the other hand, performed tasks that were "highly regimented with little operator control over work activity." The control group of non-VDT users at Blue Shield had identical jobs with the single exception that they did not use computer terminals.

The results of the survey confirm the centrality of the control issue to the problem of occupational stress. While VDT users at both the newspapers and the Blue Shield office reported health complaints such as have come to be associated with VDT work—in particular, frequent vision problems such as burning eyes, eyestrain, blurred vision, irritation, and even changes in the ability to see certain colors—the major differences were between the clerical VDT users and the other workers surveyed. "For all the significant stress factors," write the authors of the NIOSH report, "there was a similar pattern of response." The clerical VDT operators reported the highest levels of stress, followed by the non-VDT clerical workers of the control group. The professionals using the terminals as one tool among many in the course of their newspaper work reported the lowest stress levels of all.

The NIOSH researchers concluded that while VDT use did impose certain physical "stressors" that other office machines or hand work did not (for example, "the visual load of screen viewing" and "the additional postural requirements for viewing and keying"), the major factor was the *combination* of the new computer technology with the "highly regimented" organization of work in the Blue Shield office. Like Elaine Jensen, the clerical workers at Blue Shield spent the entire day before their machines. At their work stations except during formal rest breaks and lunch periods, they were monitored closely by computer, "which provided up-to-the-minute performance reports on the rate of production and error levels to supervisors." They were subject to "high production standards" and "constant pressure for performance." The workers felt "they were being 'constantly' watched by the computer and controlled by their supervisor."

The synthesis of new technology and traditional Taylorist management produced an "unusual lack of control over the work process," and this was the ultimate cause of occupational stress in the Blue Shield office. For the workers there, technology did not liberate them from the pressures and strain of the assembly line but yoked them all the tighter to a kind of mental assembly line. And the result, in the words of the NIOSH report, was "a dehumanization of work activity," "jobs that produce boredom and job dissatisfaction," and technology that "becomes a source of misery rather than a helpful tool."

Since the NIOSH VDT study was released in 1980, Blue Shield

workers at the Oakland office have seen their control over work erode even further—so far, in fact, that many have lost their jobs altogether. In preparation for contract negotiation with management in the fall of 1980, the Blue Shield clerks (members of Local 3 of the Office and Professional Employees International Union) developed some bargaining proposals about VDT work based on the NIOSH recommendations. They asked for extra breaks during the work day, "ergonomically" designed terminals and office chairs, and the end of impossible production standards. Blue Shield management denied the validity of the government health study, however, and rejected the workers' proposals. When their union contract expired in November, the Blue Shield workers decided to go out on strike.

The VDT issue was not the only disagreement between union and management. The conflict was long and bitter, lasting from November 1980 to March 1981. During the course of the strike, Blue Shield management used the tremendous flexibility that the computerization of work provides to shift much of the data-entry work done at the Oakland office to new, nonunion satellite offices in the rural Sacramento Valley nearly 150 miles away. By the end of the strike, Blue Shield workers in Oakland were able to win some of their demands, but the gains were Pyrrhic, for the work that had shifted to offices in other parts of the state during the strike never returned. What had been a workforce of some twelve hundred people at the beginning of the strike—the majority black women—was reduced to four hundred one year after its end.

Though the inability to control one's work is the major cause of occupational stress, certain other features of the new technology make that lack of control even harder for the individual to bear. The uniquely "psychological" nature of so much work in the brave new workplace may exacerbate occupational stress.

Harvard Business School professor Shoshanna Zuboff is one of the academic researchers who have been studying the special psychological requirements of what she calls "computer-mediated work." In an article in the *Harvard Business Review*, she argues that "when information technology reorganizes a job, it fundamentally alters the individual's relation to the task." What happens is that work becomes more "abstract." Instead of setting up and inspecting the operations manually, for example, a machinist monitors the performance of his machine tool (or, indeed, an entire computerized manufacturing cell) by means of his VDT screen. An engineer creates a design not with pencil, paper, compass, and ruler but on the interactive graphics display terminal of the computer-aided design system. In either case, the computerized information system intervenes between the worker and his or her work. It is the sole source of information, feedback, and control. And work becomes "the electronic manipulation of symbols" rather than a "sensual activity."

This transition to abstract work, contends Zuboff, has an enormous effect on how people feel about their jobs. She writes, "Very often . . . the object of the task seems to have disappeared 'behind the screen' and into the information system." It is as if work is somehow located "in" the computer, as if the computer itself actually does the work, not the worker. The individual is on the outside, looking in, a somewhat passive spectator. When Joe Payne describes one of the maintenance tasks that he performed on the No. 4 ESS, he starts out by saying, "What you do is—," then stops abruptly, catching himself. "Well, you don't actually *do* anything," he continues. "You just sit there and call up a list of tests; the computer does them for you." The Bell Labs technician who demonstrates the special-circuits-testing system known as SARTS puts it this way: "You're a level removed; you're seeing the operation through a shell."

According to Zuboff, this experience of being one step removed from work is very frustrating for most workers. A draftsman at the General Motors Technical Center, for example, says that when he works on the computer-aided design system, "I feel divorced from my work; it feels cold." On the other hand, just because work has become abstract does not necessarily mean that workers can do it "automatically." In fact, the very logic of computerized work—based upon the systematic application of rules encoded in computer programs —demands a unique kind of psychological investment: not "thinking" so much as "paying attention." "With computer-mediated work, patterns of attention, learning, and mental engagement become the keys to effectiveness and high-quality performance," Zuboff writes.

At the top of the occupational hierarchy, mental engagement

might mean using one's imagination to decide how best to bring the power of the computer to bear on ever more difficult, complex, and challenging tasks—the financial analyst, for example, who uses information systems to create sophisticated and up-to-date financial models. For many workers, however, it simply means knowing how and when to apply certain set computerized procedures. "In a sense, you're learning how to deal with the computer, but you don't have to know how it works," says an AT&T technician who has recently learned how to service and repair the company's "computerized branch exchange" telecommunications systems. "You have to know how to recognize certain charts and graphs, how to follow procedures. You have to be able to go by the book more." And for workers on the mental assembly line like Elaine Jensen or the clerical workers at the Oakland Blue Shield office, mental engagement means fighting to concentrate on what is essentially a mind-deadening task.

Of course, workers have always had to pay attention to their jobs. But physical work, even when unavailingly routine, allows people a kind of "mental space," a place apart where they can hold themselves in reserve. The cigar wrappers of the Manhattan lofts in the early twentieth century would listen to one of their number read from classics of literature and political thought as they repeated over and over the repetitive motions of their trade. And anyone who has ever operated a machine in a factory knows that the one advantage of a physically repetitive but essentially simple job is that it can be done almost automatically, leaving the mind free for daydreams, thoughts, and reveries. Even on the assembly line, workers can engage in conversation and social exchange, however truncated by the imperative of the moving line. These are all the little things that make work bearable; they provide the space to cope with its pressures and demands.

What Zuboff suggests is that computer-mediated work squeezes out this psychological free space. In the words of a service representative at New Jersey Bell, "it drains people in a certain way that physical labor doesn't." Even as workers feel detached from abstract work, the very nature of that work demands they invest themselves in it. And when this intrinsic tension is linked up with a radical lack of control, the inevitable result is stress. With classic academic understatement, Zuboff writes that "imposing traditional supervisory approaches on the computer-mediated environment can create considerable dysfunction." What it may really create is an enormous crisis of motivation, of efficiency, and ultimately of the work organization itself.

For the past ten years, Dr. Robert Karasek of the Department of Industrial and Systems Engineering at the University of Southern California in Los Angeles has been poring over masses of statistical data about job dissatisfaction, worker health complaints, and the occurrence of coronary heart disease and other stress-related symptoms. Studying the work and health histories of more than five thousand male workers in the United States and Sweden, he has tried to interpret the relationship between an individual's sense of control at work, the demands of his job, and occupational stress. His conclusion is that we may be witnessing "an evolution in the job structure" which will make "psychological stress . . . more prevalent."

What Karasek has done is to correlate both subjective reports and objective indicators of stress among his sample with two key occupational characteristics. The first he calls "decision latitude," the degree to which a person can exercise control on the job. Machine-pacing of work, rigid production quotas, and productivity monitoring by computer are all indications of narrow decision latitude. The ability to learn and use new skills and the authority to make decisions about how to structure one's work, on the other hand, are signs of a broader decision latitude. Karasek calls his second category "psychological demand." Time pressures to accomplish certain tasks, extensive responsibility, or the kind of mental engagement that Zuboff describes are examples of high demand. They represent the "mental load" of a job, and they indicate psychological pressure.

Survey material and epidemiological data suggest that across the occupational structure, the frequency of stress is related to the interaction of high psychological demand and a corresponding low degree of decision latitude. In effect, one can imagine all the jobs in society as located in four quadrants of a "job map." Some jobs afford workers a great deal of control while imposing few psychological demands. Compared to most occupations, these are "relaxed" jobs;

Karasek gives the examples of the librarian or dentist. The image of the traditional craftsman also comes readily to mind, or perhaps the printers of Blauner's study. In general, these workers exhibit the lowest levels of stress among all occupational groups.

Other occupations may allow for little control, but the psychological demands are also low. These are "passive" jobs—the night watchman or museum security guard. In the survey data, one finds relatively moderate stress levels among these workers as well. Interestingly enough, many jobs with low control but high *physical* demands are not particularly stressful either. In fact, robust physical activity such as that required in many traditional blue-collar jobs, as long as it is not accompanied by extensive time pressure, often protects people from stress. It may act as a kind of safety valve, a coping mechanism that liberates pent-up energy.

Still other jobs place high psychological demands on the individual but also afford a wide decision latitude. These are "active" jobs—corporate executives and brain surgeons (or, perhaps, highly skilled machinists like Dave Boggs before the Strippit 750 or the professional journalists of the NIOSH VDT study). Despite the popular image of the harried executive whose responsibilities and pressures are the bitter pill accompanying his large salary and extensive power, most survey data suggest that, in fact, symptoms of chronic stress are only average for this group. "In the 1950s and 1960s, there was a great deal of literature about executive stress syndrome," says Karasek. "What we have found is that executives' ability to exercise control at work appears to offset the heavy psychological demands they do face."

Levels of stress are the highest in jobs combining high levels of psychological demand with the inability of individuals to shape and control their work. "When we examine the full national working population" in both countries, writes Karasek, "it is primarily workers with jobs simultaneously low in job discretion and high in job demands who report exhaustion after work, trouble awakening in the morning, depression, nervousness, anxiety, and insomnia or sleep disturbance"—in short, many of the key symptoms of stress. These are the "high strain" jobs of waiters and waitresses, some assembly-line workers, and telephone operators.

If Karasek's map of the contours of occupational stress is accurate, then stress may be an intractable problem of the brave new workplace. For many of the new jobs are located in what he calls the "high strain" quadrant—the data-entry worker typing all day at her machine, the word-processing clerk whose keystrokes are counted by computer, the service representative whose telephone calls are timed to make sure she fills her quota, the telephone technician tending the computerized network. A 1984 survey of more than four thousand working women (conducted by 9 to 5, the National Association of Working Women) found that the highest incidence of frequent health problems such as headaches, nausea, digestive problems, insomnia, irritability, depression, and other indicators of stress was reported by women in automated clerical jobs.

One conceivable solution to stress would be simply to lower the level of psychological demand such workers face—in effect, to create more "passive" jobs. But, as Shoshanna Zuboff's work suggests, the unique imperatives of computer-mediated work make this impossible. Nor is simply giving workers more "responsibility" a solution. In the absence of the authority to perform one's job in the way that makes the most sense, more responsibility can lead to more dissatisfaction and stress, not less. The only real solution appears to be to organize work in a way that maximizes the control and power of the people who actually do it.

Robert Karasek's scenario of a workplace characterized by high psychological demands and low job control reaches its fullest expression where the principle of technology used as an instrument of control has been taken the farthest—in the central offices, automated service bureaus, and operator services departments of what, until January 1984, was the Bell System telecommunications network. Predictably, the Bell operating companies have experienced an outbreak of occupational stress that, in recent years, has become a serious labor-relations challenge.

The origins of AT&T's own stress epidemic go back to the major expansion of the Bell System in the late 1960s and early 1970s. As the telephone business boomed during the economic growth of the 1960s, operating companies hired thousands of new workers to fill positions in this expanding network. Many were young, part of the generation that came of age in the 1960s and was entering the workforce for the first time. Many were also women and members of minority groups, for in 1973 AT&T had signed a consent decree with the Department of Justice in order to settle an outstanding discrimination case. The corporation agreed to place more women in skilled craft jobs traditionally reserved for men, as well as substantially to increase its hiring of blacks and other minorities throughout the occupational hierarchy.

The sudden influx of this inexperienced new workforce made the issue of workplace control a sensitive one throughout the Bell System. AT&T managers relied on the traditional precepts of Taylorism to maintain managerial control over work. Increasingly, work was subjected to a new web of production standards and measures, quotas, and productivity "indexes." Whereas operating companies had once set their own work standards, this time control was centralized in AT&T corporate headquarters in New Jersey. More important, Bell System managers had computers to monitor worker performance—which made their control more total and its centralization technically more feasible. The computerization of work made possible qualitatively new forms of corporate control of work in which, according to one AT&T executive, "we can measure everything but the pressure of your left cheek on the chair."

The new technology was used in other ways that increased the tensions of telephone work. Computer systems like MLT, designed to "get people off the payroll," disrupted traditional occupational categories and skills and transformed telephone jobs. Technological change also contributed to the rapid deregulation of the telephone industry, which culminated in the divestiture of AT&T. As the various components of the Bell System moved into a more competitive economic environment, demands for higher productivity and performance increased all the more.

All these factors combined to create an incubator for occupational stress. By the end of the 1970s, rumors and stories about inordinate job pressures, pervasive alcoholism and drug abuse, even incidents of nervous breakdowns on the job were sweeping through the Bell System companies. One indication of this burgeoning stress epidemic was the growing attention and concern among telephone industry unions. Within the Communications Workers union, complaints about "job pressures" became more and more insistent. At first they came primarily from female telephone operators who worked in the most controlled and most computerized of Bell System jobs. But as new technology spread to the skilled crafts, these traditionally male (and more politically powerful) segments of the CWA membership joined the mounting chorus of complaint. CWA anxiety about occupational stress surfaced at special union conferences, meetings with management, and even testimony before the Federal Communications Commission. It culminated in a nationwide protest on June 15, 1979, known as Job Pressures Day, in which the union slogan was "We Are People, Not Machines."

At the CWA's 1980 convention in Los Angeles, a resolution condemning "service monitoring" (the measurement of employee performance by computer and other means) gave delegates an opportunity to protest what one called the "stress, abuse, and unbelievable pressure" that telephone workers were experiencing. Speakers reported increased alcoholism, tranquilizer and other drug abuse, nervous breakdowns and "stress disabilities," and forced early retirement because of high blood pressure and heart disease. One even called monitoring "a tool used by the company to force an operator into a mental state of depression." While most of the testimony focused on the plight of the telephone operator, one delegate reminded his colleagues that the problem was "spreading into other units of the system."

Meanwhile, another telephone workers' union, the Telecommunications International Union, was trying to document some of the stories about stress that staff members had been hearing in their travels around the country. In 1978, local TIU leaders in Illinois surveyed more than a thousand service representatives about stress on the job. More then half of them said it had become an "overwhelming concern." During the next two years, TIU locals all over the country distributed similar "stress surveys" with similar results. At Southern New England Telephone, for example, nearly 90 percent of more than 200 service reps said they frequently left work upset because of job pressures. Approximately 40 percent reported taking tranquilizers or other nerve medicine or increasing their consumption of alcohol, since starting on the job. And 12.3 percent were using both—a potentially lethal combination.

Faced with management challenges to the credibility of these local surveys, the TIU designed a more sophisticated survey, distributed in March 1980 to three thousand members in six states—15 percent of the union's total national membership. The 1,227 responses were also supplemented by eighty in-depth interviews. The expanded survey not only confirmed earlier reports but dramatically expressed the effects of job pressure on workers' lives. At one Bell of Pennsylvania service center, for example, it had become so bad that during a nine-month period in 1979, five out of twenty office employees had been forced off the job by work-related psychiatric disorders. The TIU Stress Report concluded that there was a "pervasive workplace atmosphere of urgency and tension" in the Bell System. "Such modern corporations as AT&T," it said, "are major sources of psychological stress."

Perhaps the most convincing sign of the stubborn stress epidemic at the Bell System was not a union study but a high-level management report. At the same time the CWA and TIU were documenting occupational stress and criticizing the extreme forms of management control that caused it, AT&T's executive-level Work Relationships Unit was coming to nearly identical conclusions. A massive corporate-wide "work relationships survey" found that nearly half of the five thousand respondents—from the lowliest operator to the highest-level manager—felt that stress on the job was worse than ever before. "After a year of digging," concluded the group's report, "we're convinced that the *central* problem is the way we manage people." Like the unionists, the managers pointed to the classic example of the telephone operator. "Operator services has been dehumanized and the workplace depersonalized by the application of technology, centralization, and the design and use of systems to manage the technology—all without sufficient recognition for their human consequences." They also admitted that the problem was not limited to operators alone. Throughout the network, there had been a "proliferation of control and micromeasurement plans." Seen from the perspective of the workplace, there was only one conclusion: "We ... give the appearance of a management that has opted for control."

One example of what can happen when management opts for control in the brave new workplace is the story of AT&T's International Operating Center in New York City. When I first visited the New York IOC in early 1981, it consisted of some 750 operators—93 percent of them women, the majority of them black—who handled an average of 24,000 calls each day to the seventy-eight foreign countries still inaccessible by direct dialing. Like operators throughout the Bell System, they exhibited some of the classic symptoms of occupational stress. Drug and alcohol use was rampant. At the time, eighteen members of CWA's Local 1150, the union representing the IOC workers, were hospitalized for substance abuse. The number of IOC workers out on "stress disability" was also unusually high. "They call them 'nervous conditions,'" explained Andrea Lupo, vice-president in charge of operator services at Local 1150. "People just get hyper. You see them; they're shaking. They can't deal with getting to work on time. They get into a fit of crying or something. One woman fainted. It's a pressure cooker in there."

What explained the stress problem in the New York IOC office? One reason was a traditional autocratic attitude on the part of local management. To give just one example, operators at the New York office (like those in Bell System operator offices all over the country) had to ask their supervisor's permission to go to the bathroom. The term for a bathroom break was a "run-out." An operator would call her supervisor in order to get on the run-out waiting list. Sometimes the wait could be as long as an hour. And when her turn finally arrived, it was important not to dally. Bathroom visits were timed by management.

When the new computerized system for connecting overseas calls was introduced in the office in 1979, workers had hoped it would alleviate some of the harsher forms of management control. In fact, it only made things worse. The new VDTs of the international operating system allowed supervisors to monitor office performance by computer in automatic fifteen-minute intervals. And computerization of the office scheduling system permitted managers to indulge their penchant for control even more.

Before the introduction of the computerized scheduling system, about half the operators were guaranteed what was known as a "basic tour"—the same work hours each day for two weeks. But computerization allowed management to estimate the number of operators needed at any particular moment of the day more accurately and to schedule the workforce more tightly. So, in the interests of office "flexibility," the number of operators receiving basic tours was cut to 35 percent. But what made for the flexibility of the office as a whole meant substantial disruption for individual IOC workers. Without a basic tour, operators could be scheduled to fill different time periods each day, as the office workflow demanded. Some operators no longer needed on the newly efficient day tour were transferred to nights. Veterans with twenty years' experience suddenly found they had to start working Saturdays again. Others found that the computer was scheduling their fifteen-minute morning break a brief forty-five minutes after they arrived for work. "Before, you could get some order into your life," said one New York IOC operator. "But they want workers flexible—like puppets. They want them dangling around every day."

The use of tranquilizers and other prescription drugs is common practice in many Bell System offices, and the New York IOC was no exception. However, according to workers at Local 1150, workplace drug abuse was given a substantial boost by the AT&T medical office. "The company indiscriminately precribes drugs to its employees," Don Collins, who had set up a special counseling referral. program at the local to assist workers with drug and alcohol problems, told me soon after I began visiting the New York IOC. He and other workers described case after case where the company medical personnel, usually nurses, distributed small quantities of Valium, Darvon, codeine, and other drugs, in unmarked envelopes and without prescriptions—a practice that was possibly illegal and potentially dangerous.

According to Collins, one employee just out of the hospital after a bout of alcoholism was givenValium for her nerves. Only after the union complained did the medical department agree to mark its records to make sure that workers with histories of alcoholism or drug abuse never received Valium again. Another employee was prescribed Valium for nearly a year and a half; then, when his work performance began to deteriorate because of his dependence on the drug, he was threatened with disciplinary action. "Our opinion was they were building a case to get rid of him," says Don Collins. Fortunately, this time there was a written prescription, signed by a company doctor. When Collins and his union colleague Bill McIntyre presented it to management, the company backed down. "They wanted to indict him as a junkie," remembers McIntyre, "and we were indicting them as the pusher."

At one point, the job pressures at the New York IOC even boiled over into a bitter labor conflict. In December 1979, office workers went out on a three-day unauthorized wildcat strike right before the Christmas holiday. No ordinary walkout, the Christmas strike was a rank-and-file protest against workplace stress. During the preceding year, the 1,000-operator workforce had been cut through attrition and dismissals to 850. Suspensions and dismissals were mounting; oversupervision grew more severe. "They were monitoring us constantly," remembers Andrea Lupo. "It was driving us up the wall."

In September, the new computerized scheduling system was introduced and immediately made a mess of office scheduling. Then, on December 14, Catherine Daily, a sixty-two-year-old operator who had worked at the New York IOC since she was twenty-five, died of a heart attack that many of her co-workers thought was job-related. A few days before, Daily had been suspended for the first time in her thirty-six years with the telephone company when she had briefly "plugged out" her position while filling out a repair ticket. When she returned to work the next day, she was nervous and upset; she complained that her supervisor was watching her every move. When Daily died, she was only a few weeks from retirement.

A week after Daily's death, nearly three-quarters of the office's operators walked off the job. From December 21 to December 23, a picket line blocked the main entrance to the IOC building on the Avenue of the Americas. A coffin was set up at the building entrance; its epitaph read "Job Pressures Are Killing Our Members." Workers handed out leaflets to the milling crowd of curious Christmas shoppers and Lower Manhattan office workers. They also staged mock mourning rituals before the coffin, complete with crying and wailing. Meanwhile, back at the Local 1150 union hall three blocks away on Broadway, workers were discovering a sense of community and power they had rarely experienced on the job. Union members ran a day-care center to look after operators' children so mothers could walk the picket line. When evening came, instead of going home, day-shift workers went to the union hall for a quick dinner and then returned to the nonstop demonstration in the street.

Desperate to end the walkout before the heavy long-distance traffic of Christmas Eve, AT&T went to court. On December 23, the U.S. District Court for the Southern District of New York issued an injunction ordering striking operators back to work. "It was a very emotional time," Andrea Lupo remembers. "Everybody was crying. We didn't want to go back." But union leaders were hesitant to defy the injunction. Instead, they urged their members to return to work, but "not like meek little lambs." So, on the day before Christmas, the operators of the New York IOC returned to their video display terminals, sporting stickers reading "Forced by the Feds" and, not long after the seizure of the American hostages in Iran, "Held Hostage by AT&T."

The Christmas strike was an emotional catharsis, an antidote to the powerlessness that so many of the New York IOC operators felt. But it did not solve their occupational stress problem. The ultimate solution came a few years later in a manner that few of the workers expected or welcomed. In August 1982, AT&T announced the closing of the New York IOC, ostensibly because of technological advances in the international operating system. Some workers were able to transfer to other jobs in the Bell System. Others chose early retirement; still others "voluntarily" left the company, with severance pay. Nevertheless, in July 1983, some three hundred of the remaining IOC workers were permanently laid off without special benefits of any kind. Finally, on December 12, 1983, almost a full four years after the Christmas strike, the New York City International Operating Center was permanently closed, its occupational stress problem eliminated once and for all.

Worker protests against occupational stress, like the New York Christmas strike, are relatively rare. "People don't normally fight back," says a CWA shop steward at a Washington, D.C., operator office, "and it builds up inside them until it comes out in headaches or breakdowns." It's not that people don't realize the pressures confronting them at work. The problem is, they blame themselves. Stress corrodes their sense of self. More than just a lack of control over work, it signals an inability to cope with the demands of their world. "Workers recognize they are facing stress," explains Dr. Michael Lerner, a clinical psychologist and director of the Institute for Labor and Mental Health in Oakland, California, one of the few worker-oriented stress centers in the country. "Nevertheless, they see it as their own inability to function according to the norms established by the company. They feel they are individually failing to live up."

Thus, occupational stress can eventually come to color an individual's entire life. "It would get into your blood," says a telephone worker who suffered two nervous breakdowns as a result of the pressures of her service representative job. "I would go home depressed and cry a lot. On weekends, I didn't want to do anything; all I could do was think about my job. I felt like I was failing. I worried about breaking down at work, because nobody knew what I was going through. I wanted to do the job right—for them, but also for me. I didn't want to screw up." Job pressures finally forced her out of her Bell System service representative job. And yet, years later, she still finds it hard to blame anyone but herself. The engineers who established the work standards in her office were unknown to her. What she remembers about her immediate supervisors was their concern. "They couldn't have been more considerate," she says. "They're in the same boat as you are."

Ironically, the very impersonality of control in the computerized workplace—the fact that it resides in no specific manager but is the product of some shadowy and intangible "system"—evokes a highly personal response. And because people tend to take the erosion of their control over work so personally, more often than not they retreat into a passive immobility rather than embrace rebellion and press for change. This reinforces the very relations of power that produce occupational stress in the first place.

But there is a second irony here as well: this immobility is a dilemma not merely for the individual worker but for the corporation as a whole. For despite the technology managers' dream of a perfectly functioning automatic workplace, work remains a social activity. And the skills, attitudes, and motivations of workers remain crucial to effective work performance and corporate success.

At the very center of these managerial visions of control lies a worrisome contradiction. It is one to which more and more managers of the brave new workplace are anxiously trying to respond.

PART TWO

THE REENCHANTMENT OF THE WORKPLACE

CHAPTER FOUR

———

THE HUMAN CONNECTION

———

THE TECHNOLOGIES TRANSFORMING WORKING LIFE may be new and relatively unfamiliar, but the conflicts over control they have inspired certainly are not. Indeed, these conflicts constitute the most recent version of a story that has been more than a century in the telling: how society defines authority in the workplace and how those definitions reflect the contest of conflicting social interests. Behind the computerization of work in the brave new workplace lies the ongoing evolution of that system of authority and social control that we have come to know as modern "management."

Usually we tend to think of management as an unchanging and inevitable given in any work organization. But the origin of the idea of management is actually quite recent. It dates from around the turn of the century, during another period of enormous change in working life, not all that dissimilar in form from what is taking place today. Then, as now, work was buffeted by a variety of social, economic, and technological forces. The market economy was spreading, and entering into more and more areas of social life. New technologies based on coal, steel, and electricity were being commercially exploited. Corporations were growing larger and organizationally more complex. And new groups of workers, former agricultural laborers and European immigrants, were entering the workplace.

All these changes served to challenge traditional conceptions of authority at work, based on the model of the individual capitalist entrepreneur whose power was justified by the "natural rights" of property and whose relationship with his workforce was either authoritarian or paternalist (usually some combination of the two).

As change undermined the foundations of this earlier model, companies were forced to articulate a new set of principles for organizing their control over work, a new way of explaining and justifying what they did. It was the birth of the idea of "management."

The concept of management represented a new way of understanding and organizing human behavior. It saw authority not as a function of mutual obligations and personal ties, but as the product of a rational and impersonal system. And the justification for this new managerial authority was not the quasi-religious notion of "natural rights" but the rational and supremely scientific idea of efficiency.

One of the first persons to recognize the special logic of management was the German social theorist Max Weber. Writing at the turn of the century, he identified the constituent elements of an emerging social form. In the armed forces, in government and political administration, but most of all in "the most advanced institutions of industrial capitalism," a distinctive mode of social organization was coming to the fore and systematically stamping its indelible imprint on human behavior and social life. Weber's term for this social form was "bureaucracy."

For Weber, bureaucracy was different from earlier models of social organization based upon traditional religious values or the "charismatic" authority of a personal leader, because it operated according to the principle of "instrumental rationality." Bureaucracy was dedicated to the methodical achievement of practical results. Whatever the specific goals of the organization (whether to win a war, to ensure the political power of a social class, or to make a profit in the marketplace), the formal means of a bureaucracy were always the same: the precise specialization of tasks and functions; the creation of explicit hierarchies of control to wield those functions into a coherent whole; and the articulation of "calculable rules" defining duties and qualifications for the people who would occupy the various positions in the bureaucratic organization.

Bureaucratic control maximized predictability, minimized ambiguity, and carefully matched means to ends. And it did so without regard to questions of ultimate value or to the influence of personal loyalties or attachments. According to Weber, it was a "precision instrument" for the calculated pursuit of predetermined ends.

The metaphor is appropriate, for Weber's model of bureaucracy was that of a smooth-functioning machine. Bureaucracy compared to more traditional forms of social organization, he wrote, "exactly as does the machine with the nonmechanical modes of production." Administration and management founded upon instrumental rationality made the control of human behavior entirely a matter of technique. And the justification for that control was strictly utilitarian—what Weber described as the "purely technical superiority" of bureaucracy over "any other form of organization."

This mechanical mode of social organization reached its fullest expression in the principles and practices of scientific management. "Organizational discipline in the factory," Weber wrote, "is founded upon a completely rational basis. With the help of the appropriate methods of measurement"—like the time and motion studies of Taylorism—"the optimum profitability of the individual worker is calculated like that of any material means of production." And, for this reason, "the American system of 'scientific management' enjoys the greatest triumphs in the rational conditioning and training of work performance."

In effect, scientific management remade individuals in the image and likeness of the machine. The very "psycho-physical apparatus of man" was "completely adjusted to the demands of the outer world, the tools, the machines—in short, to an individual function." And the individual worker was "shorn of his natural rhythm as determined by the structure of the organism" in order to become "attuned to a new rhythm through a methodical specialization."

Even as he documented the increasing dominance of instrumental rationality in social and economic life, however, Weber was profoundly ambivalent about its consequences. On the one hand, the efficiency and organizational power of bureaucracy, manifested at every turn, was undermining traditional forms of social organization and domination and destroying the antiquated values on which they were based. There was little question in his mind that it would become the dominant social form in modern society. And yet, the very machinelike and unrelentingly utilitarian quality of bureaucratic control brought with it a corrosive depersonalization of social life— what Weber called (borrowing a phrase from the nineteenth-century German philosopher Friedrich Schiller) "the disenchantment of the world." As the imperative of instrumental rationality tied more and more people to vast hierarchical organizations and defined them in terms of narrow impersonal functions within those organizations, bureaucracy reshaped how they worked and how they behaved, how they perceived the world and what they valued in it. It progressively drained the sense of purpose and meaning from social life. The price of bureaucracy's triumph was to trap human civilization in an "iron cage" of undifferentiated routine and impersonal calculation.

Weber understood that bureaucracy could become a structure of domination, a means for specific social groups or classes to pursue their own interests at the expense of others. The advocates of scientific management, however, took Weber's analytical concept of "instrumental rationality" and turned it into an ideological principle. They transformed the idea of "management," with its logic of efficiency and control, into something much closer to its conventional meaning today—a universal value. The "science" of management became equated with human progress.

In particular, scientific management was presented as the solution to the bitter class conflicts that had shaped the industrial workplace during the Industrial Revolution. It became the key to a kind of industrial utopia where all conflict would cease and work organizations would function as smoothly as a well-regulated machine. "Under scientific management," Frederick Taylor told a special Congressional committee in 1911, "arbitrary power . . . ceases; and . . . every single subject, large and small, becomes a question of scientific investigation, for reduction to law." This equation of "rationalization" with "rationality" was supposed to eliminate all possibility of dispute between employers and workers. Indeed, under scientific management, Taylor argued, "the men who were formerly called bosses . . . become the servants of the workmen." In exchange for ceding the control of work to these impartial experts, workers would share in the enormous productivity gains that scientific management made possible. Managerial control would mean higher wages and a new era of consensus, not only at work but in society as a whole. In this respect, Taylor claimed, "scientific management is a true democracy."

Of course, it was nothing of the sort. The Taylorist system of management did not eliminate the clash of conflicting interests in the workplace—let alone in society. It only disguised those conflicts behind the standards and practices of impersonal and ostensibly scientific technique. At first, the introduction of scientific management (in the early decades of the twentieth century) sparked severe labor conflicts, as workers, in particular skilled craftsmen, fought against the systematic erosion of autonomy that this new managerial system meant for them. By the 1930s, outright rebellion had given way to an uneasy accommodation. Resistance to scientific management took the form of informal efforts by small work groups to turn the standards of scientific management to their own ends—by systematically restricting output and setting quotas for "making out."

These and other problems led some business thinkers and corporate managers to distance themselves from the claims that Taylor had made for scientific management. They argued that the model of bureaucratic rationality and efficiency articulated by Weber and applied to the workplace by Taylor was incomplete. It was so mechanistic that it ignored the nonrational "human" dimension of work. From the "welfare capitalism" of the 1920s to Elton Mayo's "human relations" school of management in the 1930s to "group dynamics" and "organizational development" in the 1950s and 1960s, some managers have tried to develop practices that would humanize "scientific management" and tap the tremendous energy of informal social relations in the workplace to the benefit of the corporation. They made the same utopian claims for their systems as Taylor did for his at the beginning of the century. And, like Taylor, they promised to put an end to conflict at work.

Whatever the degree of interest in such initiatives at any moment in time, however, "humanistic" management always remained a distinctly subordinate point of view, more a supplement to Taylorism than an alternative to it. Instead of rejecting the logic of instrumental rationality, it sought methods for applying that logic to the more intractable realms of human behavior. Thus, according to

Mayo, the human relations school was simply "a new method of human control." As a result, humanistic management ended up as little more than a safety valve for managing worker discontent and the human problems that Taylorism invariably created.

Even industrial unionism, by far the most effective defense for workers against the depersonalization of scientific management, served to reinforce the logic of efficiency and control in the workplace. Collective bargaining helped to ameliorate the most serious abuses of bureaucratic control. It forced management to negotiate work rules and standards. It established detailed seniority systems regulating how workers moved through the bureaucratic hierarchy of the workplace. Perhaps most important, it became the mechanism by which corporations were finally made to deliver on the promise of increased wages that was an integral part of the Taylorist ideology earlier in the century.

But there were strict limits to unionism's effect or influence. Ultimately, organized labor was forced to accept the corporation's control over the organization of work and technology (through the "management's rights" clauses that became a standard part of most union contracts). In doing so, they ceased to challenge the fundamental premise of corporate management. Industrial unionism transformed scientific management from a managerial ideology into an industrial relations system, what Daniel Bell in 1956 called a "cult of efficiency" reigning over working life.

And yet, hardly more than a decade later, this managerial system was facing a serious and multifaceted crisis. It first became apparent in the 1960s and early 1970s, when a series of workplace revolts (the best-known being the 1974 wildcat strike at the General Motors Assembly Division in Lordstown, Ohio) brought the issue of worker dissatisfaction into the public consciousness. At the time, most observers interpreted these rebellions as the reaction of a new generation of workers, shaped by the economic prosperity of the 1950s and the social movements of the 1960s, to the constraints of bureaucracy. For example, the pollster Daniel Yankelovich began talking about the "new rules" that this generation of younger workers was bringing to working life—in particular, the idea that work should be something more than just a job, that it could be an occasion for self-development and personal expression.

Before long, these social concerns about worker alienation were joined by the fear that in a more strenuous global economic environment, these new social values might impede the competitiveness of American business. In a study entitled "Work and Human Values: An International Report on Jobs in the 1980s and 1990s," Yankelovich and an international team of social scientists worried that the new rules might be "out of synchrony with the imperative of economic competition." "At the same time that the industrialized democracies are facing the most severe economic challenges," they wrote, "their citizens seem less willing than in the past to make the sacrifices that may be needed to meet those challenges." Thus, what under conditions of relative prosperity had been a distressing but relatively manageable problem now became a potentially dangerous crisis of motivation.

This is the context in which the computerization of work, described in Part One, has taken place. At first glance, the new technology seems to be the culmination of instrumental rationality and managerial control at work. Indeed, many managers have seen it as the perfect tool for the reassertion of their control. But the psychological and organizational costs of this rigid managerial control confront managers with an unexpected dilemma. Not only can computerization exacerbate alienation and dissatisfaction in the workplace, but in its destruction of the very human qualities on which the effective performance of work tasks so often depends, it can also be surprisingly inefficient. Thus, the new technology that was supposed to be the perfect technical solution to the crisis of managerial authority in working life has become a considerable managerial problem in its own right.

This contradiction has given birth to an extraordinary irony. Precisely at the moment when the workplace is becoming more rationalized, more technologically intensive, more automated and more controlled, managers are turning their attention to the irrational side of working life and making the ineffable realm of human values and motivations the conspicuous object of their concern. They are attempting to define yet another utopian language of management whose key words are not so much "rationalization" and "control" but "trust" and "commitment," "participation" and "humanization."

Where Max Weber warned of the "disenchantment of the world" brought about by the "iron cage" of bureaucracy, they seem to promise a "reenchantment" of the brave new workplace and the intricately orchestrated infusion of meaning into working life.

An important area for this reenchantment of work is technology itself. As some managers grasp the contradictions of control in the brave new workplace, they are beginning to see the Taylorist use of new technology as an obstacle to the successful computerization of work.

Consider some of the comments at the annual office automation trade show of the American Federation of Information Processing Societies, held in San Francisco in April 1982. Like previous office technology fairs, this one was replete with eye-catching displays and fancy demonstrations, but it had an extra dimension as well. Its theme was "The Human Connection," and, far from celebrating technology's pending triumph over the human element at work, it warned that the very future of the brave new workplace depended not on the hardware and software of the computer but on the subtle and confusing vagaries of human behavior.

The trade fair chairman, Hans Puehse, described what he called "the dilemma many office managers and corporate planners face"— not whether to go ahead with the computerization of work but whether "potential systems users" could overcome their "fears associated with change." Another speaker urged companies to "combine office automation with office humanization" before it was too late. A third warned darkly that employee resistance to new technology could become the "Achilles' heel" of the long-awaited Information Age.

The perils of ignoring this "human connection" have become an increasingly common theme among some technology managers.

"The real problems facing us are not technological," says Fred Portner, a Houston banker responsible for office automation projects. "They're human-behavior-oriented. We have the technology but we don't change the managerial and organizational culture in order to use it properly. We just slug it into the existing culture."

And, in language that would win the immediate and whole-hearted assent of a Dave Boggs or a Joe Payne, technology consultant Peter Keen has written: "The systems-development Fiasco Hall of Fame is packed with examples of costly mistakes, costly in terms of disruption and morale, not just money, caused by tenacious ignorance regarding users and their world. . . . The technocentric tradition has largely led to a naive view of the user, simplistic concepts of work, overmechanized and inflexible models of organizational and social processes, and, above all, a definition of 'productivity' in terms of the ethos of efficiency."

The problems created by this ignorance of "users and their world" are many. The one most technology managers mention, as the comments from the "human connection" conference suggest, is employee resistance to technological change. "Resistance" is the nightmare on the far side of the technology managers' dream of control. They come back to it, again and again, trading horror stories about resistance like Boy Scouts telling ghost stories around a campfire.

One veteran systems designer relates "an old war story" from his days at IBM. He was installing a "computer time-management" system at a small machine shop, designed to automate the process by which employees kept track of the amount of time they worked on each job. In the well-known tradition, as soon as the system was running smoothly, the company laid off the person who had manually tabulated the timecards. However, the laid-off worker also happened to be the union shop steward. The workers' anger, the designer remembers, was taken out on the computer.

"They just sabotaged it," he says, shaking his head with the disbelief that has lingered through the years, "just absolutely sabotaged it. And not just by making errors and stuff. They did actual physical damage." One driver of the shop hi-lo, for example, occasionally ran into the shop-floor terminal—"accidentally," of course. "They destroyed the machines," says the designer. "That can happen if you don't implement the technology properly."

Of course, resistance need not always be so organized or so blatant. The clerk in the Citibank bank-card processing center who hangs up on a customer in order to make sure the call comes in under the two-minute time limit is also engaging in a kind of resistance. So is the insurance claims processor who types fictional data into her terminal in order to make her electronic quota for the day. Resistance can also take the form of the consistent underutilization of equipment—the middle manager, for example, who avoids using the centralized word-processing pool because he prefers his own secretary. And as more and more corporations use technology to reorganize managerial jobs, resistance can even reach into the upper levels of the work organization. Whatever its precise form, it can mean enormous costs to the firm.

Most technology managers talk ambiguously about resistance. While they recognize it as a management problem, something to guard against and to avoid, they tend to blame the workers. When people resist technology, the presumption goes, they are being short-sighted; they are opposing "progress" and "change." Their behavior may be understandable (the natural fear of the unknown) but it certainly isn't rational. Others realize, however, that what people are really resisting is not so much technology itself as the system of authority that treats people as a mere adjunct to the machine. Through resistance, however informal or even unconscious, they are challenging the legitimacy of managerial control itself.

"The technology is used as a power ploy," says one systems designer at a major office technology manufacturer. "People resent it like hell and I don't blame them." Currently, he continues, some mangers see the use of technology to expand managerial power as "the wave of the future. But in a few years, after a few major disasters happen, the problems are going to be there for all to see. Why, it could serve to unionize most American office workers over the next five years!"

And yet, resistance is only the most visible cost of ignoring the human connection. Even before new computer systems reach the shop floor, the attitudes and assumptions that see technology exclusively as a "technical" issue can also affect—and distort—the very process of "systems design" itself.

Steve Taylor's story about Texas International illustrates how computerization depends on a man-made model of what goes on in the workplace. It is the responsibility of the systems designer to make sure that this model, encoded in the programs of the computer, is an accurate one. In this, designers are dependent on the very people whose work they plan to automate.

However, if office work is contingent on informal and unstructured "practical action" to the degree that the Xerox research described in Chapter 2 indicates, then tapping people's knowledge about their work is not always so easy as Taylor's description of what happened at Texas International might suggest. If a designer isn't careful, he can end up doing what Beau Sheil, a cognitive psychologist and manager for product development at Xerox Artificial Intelligence Systems, calls "automating a fiction."

Sheil is referring neither to the tendency of some managers to view technology as an instrument of control nor to that of some workers to resist this erosion of their own autonomy at work. In fact, the dangers of automating a fiction are immensely more complicated because they are founded on an unconscious and unexpressed conflict of perspectives present in most system design projects and shared by even the best-intentioned of designers and the most cooperative of workers. According to Sheil, there is a gap in world views between those who design the new technology and those who use it. The designer and office worker are like foreigners speaking different languages, with the added complication that each of them uses the same words to mean entirely different things.

On the one side of this epistemological divide, the designer, trained in the traditions of computer science, sees the development of new workplace systems as a more or less clear-cut technical problem. For him, the purpose of his work is to give office work "procedures" a precise, technical content, to define them as elements in an unambiguous, step-by-step process capable of being mimicked in a computer program. Thus, he tries to determine exactly how people do their work—devising elaborate interview methodologies, winning their cooperation, and asking probing questions.

On the other side of the divide, the office worker is constantly providing outsiders with descriptions of what she does, in order to obtain some appropriate piece of information or resolve some administrative difficulty. For her, the concept of work "procedures" has an entirely different meaning, far more open-ended and flexible. They are shorthand symbols for her tasks, rather than detailed descriptions of the tasks themselves.

What often happens, says Beau Sheil, is that the designer—against his will and much to his dismay—finds himself participating in the very social system he is supposed to be rationalizing. No matter how careful his questions or how elaborate his methodology or how cautious his cultivation of worker cooperation, he finds that office workers behave toward him exactly as they would toward anyone approaching them for information about their work. "They tell you what *they* think you need to know," says Sheil, "but it can still have nothing to do with reality"—the reality of how they *really* do their work. In fact, because "practical action" is by definition informal and unarticulated, office workers are often not conscious of it and cannot objectively describe it, no matter how cooperative they may want to be. As a result, "there is a colossal mind-clash happening at this very moment in the offices of America," concludes Sheil. "It's the systems-people versus the people."

Beau Sheil conceives the design of new workplace technology as a complicated social process. Indeed, it is a conversation where misunderstandings abound and authentic communication is achieved only with difficulty. The good systems designer needs to be something of an anthropologist as well as a computer programmer or engineer. He must be adept at moving between two social worlds. And it would help matters considerably if office workers had a modicum of technical knowledge that would allow them to grasp the logic of computer systems, so that they would have a clear sense of what kind of information the designer needs.

As long as technology managers cling to a narrowly "technocentric" approach, they will miss the subtle problems associated with applying computer technology to human work. And they will continue to create technological systems that not only trap workers in narrow and rigid jobs but also obstruct the creation of truly efficient work organizations. "What worries me, as a systems designer," says Sheil, "is that we are casting the informal office in a kind of technical cement. And it's quite likely that we're going to get it wrong."

Even when computer systems are well designed and successfully implemented, there is still another set of problems that ignoring the human connection can engender. The full advantages of new technology often go unrealized because managers overestimate how automatic these systems will be and underestimate the skills and training workers require in order to operate them effectively.

One version of this dilemma is when managers misjudge the continuing importance of certain traditional work skills in the new automated environment. Remember the story of the Bell System's MLT, told in Chapter 2. Designed to "get people off the payroll"—specifically, the highly skilled test-desk technician—MLT had some unintended consequences: the very sophistication of the system introduced new levels of complexity and vulnerability into the line-testing process and caused new errors. As a result, management found that it could not eliminate the test-desk technician entirely (although, in some Bell operating companies, their wages were cut).

There is growing evidence that the Taylorist approach to new technology also underestimates the qualitatively new skills that the "abstract" work of computer-based systems can require—and even in what seem to be the most clerical and routine of jobs.

Consider the example of a teller working in a branch office of a major bank.* Before the introduction of an on-line information system, a customer would come in to deposit or cash a check or make some other transaction, the teller would fill out a form or stamp the check, and this documentation would then travel through a whole series of offices where still other workers would process the records of the transaction and enter them into the bank's accounts—a process that might take a matter of days.

In a fully computerized bank, however, the "span" of the teller's

---

* This example is drawn from a paper entitled "New Technologies, New Skills" by Paul Adler of the Stanford School of Engineering.

job is considerably broadened. He simply enters the transaction into the computer by means of the computer terminal right at the counter. And the moment he enters the information—the customer's name and account number, the amount of the transaction, his own personal identification code, and so on—it immediately travels through all the different data bases of the bank, in what technology mangers call "real time." Instead of passing through many workers, the entire process requires only one. And what took days in the manual system now proceeds immediately through the multiple information systems of the bank, like a long row of falling dominoes, making changes in records and affecting electronic funds transfers.

This change creates considerable new responsibilities for that teller at the counter. Because he is no longer backed up by an army of "back-office" clerks who process his transactions (and, often, catch his mistakes), it becomes *extremely* important that he get the information right the first time. True, there are elaborate internal checks within the computer system; special programs automatically review the entry to make sure that the teller has the authority to make the transaction indicated and that it is "internally consistent." But while such systems can minimize "human error," they can never entirely eliminate it. And should the teller make a mistake—in the amount of money on the check, for example—that mistake gets recorded, just like any other entry, in all the information records of the bank. Errors may be less frequent in the computerized workplace, but they are far more serious when they do occur. It becomes the weighty responsibility of the worker to avoid them.

Because the teller is on the front line, so to speak, of a complex network of information systems, he also has to understand how the information system itself works and how the bank's services and functions are organized. Suppose that while the teller is entering the information for a particular transaction, the screen suddenly goes blank and the computer goes down. This is relatively common; sometimes, it happens only for a few seconds. Should he continue from where he left off or begin the transaction all over again? How does he know whether or not he is duplicating information already in the system—information that, ultimately, is going to determine how much money the customer is said to have in his or her account? To know the answer one must know how the system works, what its capabilities are, and what to do when something goes wrong—crucial technical knowledge.

Suppose that a customer comes in to complain about a transaction made the previous month which has gone unrecorded on his statement. The teller has to know where the mistake may have been made in the system and how to track it down. Efficient service depends upon his working knowledge not only of his own job but of the entire work system of the bank—attributes that the Taylorist approach is especially ill suited to encourage.

The problem of "resistance," the long-term danger of "automating a fiction," the qualitatively new demands of computerized work—all these seem to contradict the imperative of management control. In the computerized workplace, workers need *more* access to information, more training in both computer systems and work organization, more integrated jobs, and more autonomy and discretion over how technology is organized and used. Most of all, the effective computerization of work depends upon *motivated* workers who are willing to adapt to new technology, to perform their jobs responsibly, to persist in the face of abstract tasks.

This basic insight has inspired a new language of technology management whose prime focus of attention is the "user." Its proponents champion "user-friendly" software (which adapts technology to the needs of the worker rather than the other way around) and praise the virtues of "user participation" (which involves workers in the design and implementation of new technical systems). Instead of concentrating on technology's ability to eliminate human work, they emphasize its potential as a "support tool" that will turn disaffected secretaries and clerical workers into committed "knowledge workers." Finally, they suggest that success in the brave new workplace may ultimately depend not on the hardware and software of the computer but on what a memo from Bell Labs calls "roleware"—the ability of companies to create the proper attitudes for effective work in the computerized workplace.

The Houston banker Fred Portner puts it this way: "You would think that high productivity and the use of technology would depersonalize the work environment. And, initially, that's probably what happened. But now, we're looking at technology more ingeniously. We're using it to repersonalize the workplace."

The message of the human connection sounds like so much common sense. Why not use new technology to give people more control over their work, to make work more satisfying rather than less, and in the process to improve the quality of jobs and the effectiveness of the work organization itself? It is not surprising that some managers, when they come up against the limitations of the Taylorist model for work and technology, have developed an alternative approach based on the centrality of the human connection. However, this potential solution to the contradictions of control in the brave new workplace contains a delicate and far from theoretical dilemma all its own. If technology managers loosen their control over the computerization of work, might this not threaten managerial power in the workplace as a whole?

In an article on the managerial challenge of the Information Age, Xerox vice-president Paul Strassman touches on this dilemma. "The practical manager," writes Strassman, "could easily point to an enormous potential for abuse where controls have been diminished and where individuals misuse their discretionary powers." The solution, according to Strassman, is to replace the crude and increasingly ineffective mechanisms of bureaucratic control with a far more sophisticated alternative. As he writes, "Social history and anthropology point to the exceedingly effective application of social support—as a reward—and social sanction—as a deterrent—to drive toward social stability in the workplace."

Put another way, "repersonalizing" work requires something more than merely paying attention to the social dimensions of technological change. It also entails inducing workers to participate in (to "take personally") a new system of authority at work. Of course, how participation is defined (and by whom) will determine what that authority system looks like. While "social stability" may be a goal to which almost everyone can subscribe, one can imagine many different ideas about what constitutes stability and how best to achieve it.

Consider the example of "user participation." It is the idea that if the design and implementation of new workplace technical systems is to be effective, the users of the technology need to be involved. In recent years, user participation has become part of the new conventional wisdom about how to manage technological change. Researchers and technology vendors have touted it as a way to combine the smooth implementation of new technology with the creation of more satisfying jobs. (One technique of user participation, developed at the Digital Equipment Corporation, is even known as ETHICS, for Effective Technical and Human Implementation of Computer-based Systems.)

But, of course, what user participation really means depends on how one defines the "user." Here, some of the problems of the human connection begin to arise. More often than not, user participation as practiced by many technology vendors does not involve workers at all. What these firms really mean by user participation is the involvement of office managers who supervise the use of new technical systems.

And even when workers do participate in technology projects, there is another common limitation. "Users" are defined primarily in terms of the functions they perform. The fact that these users are also people who bring particular goals and interests to the workplace which may be different from or even conflict with those of management is rarely considered a legitimate concern.

Thus, when we turn from recent criticisms of the "technocentric" approach to examine how technology managers are actually using the ideas of the human connection, it becomes clear that their goal of repersonalizing the workplace has stringent limits. As a result, workers are often forced to participate in a system of power and authority over which they have little influence or control.

When I asked for examples of workplaces shaped by "the human connection," some of the managers I talked to mentioned an experiment in technological change and work redesign that took place at the "back-office" processing center of Citibank at 111 Wall Street in New York City. Known by the profoundly suggestive name "Paradise," the project has acquired a considerable reputation as an example of the office of the future and as a case study in the consummate management of technological change. Paradise has been described in the pages of the *Harvard Business Review*. Citibank has even made a film about it. The Wall Street back office has been featured in the *New York Times* as the archetypal "workplace of the future" and praised in MIT's prestigious *Technology Review* as "a showcase of bureaucracy revamped." Most important of all, Paradise has attracted near-legendary status among bankers eager to cash in on the Information Age. "Have you talked to Matteis?" asks Fred Portner in Houston, referring to the Citibank vice-president who organized the Paradise project. "He is among the few who really understand the dynamics of how to automate an office."

In the mid-1970s, Richard Matteis, in charge of clerical operations at what was then Citibank's International Group on Wall Street, faced what seemed to be an insurmountable problem. At the time, the Wall Street back office was what Matteis calls "a tremendous paper factory." The vertiginous expansion of banking services during the 1960s had pushed back-office employment and labor costs to record levels. Between 1960 and 1970, Citibank's internal operating costs were increasing at a rate of 15 percent per year. In a classic example of what technology consultant Peter Keen calls "diseconomies of administration," the more business the bank attracted, the higher the unit costs of doing the business became. By the 1970s, this explosion of people and paper was threatening to get out of control.

At the same time, work in the Citibank back office suffered from the worst features of a Taylorist work organization. "Traditionally, banks have been extremely conservative institutions," says a technical consultant to the bank during the years of the Paradise project. "It's almost like a military organization. You have your 'officers,' the senior managers, and your 'men,' the line supervisors and clerical workers." The Wall Street facility had always been a magnet for the dead-end jobs at the low end of the occupational hierarchy.

All the international processing for the bank was divided among functional departments—one each for letters of credit, money transfers, and other bank services. The processing for each particular service was further subdivided into discrete, fragmented tasks. In the letter-of-credit department (where the first experiments in work re-design took place), some thirty different processing steps were per-formed by fourteen people in order to issue a single letter. The process took about five days (and umpteen forms, tickets, and files) to complete. There were ten different job titles in the department. And should some overseas customer make the mistake of trying to find out the status of his request for a letter of credit, there was an entirely separate customer service department with the unenviable task of tracking down the letter in this bureaucratic maze.

Needless to say, jobs in the back office were not particularly challenging. "You used to do one job continuously," says one letter-of-credit department worker. "You could go a little crazy it was so boring." Motivation and morale were low. And the fact that workers handled only one fragment of the entire job meant that errors were common and tended to accumulate as a letter passed through the long issuing process. At one point, a backlog of some 36,000 cus-tomer inquiries had collected in the system.

To Citibank managers, the obvious solution was to automate. The first reaction, Matteis recalls, was "Let's turn it into an assembly line." The bank brought in a new group of managers from the Ford Motor Company, well versed in the methods and principles of indus-trial automation. They used computer technology to recreate in the office the standardized workflows of the factory. "Control was the focal point of this organization change," Matteis writes in the *Har-vard Business Review,* "the kind of control ensured by the production management disciplines applied in manufacturing concerns." In other words, the Citibank managers started with the classic techno-centric approach. They focused on improving productivity by cut-ting labor costs and better controlling the work process.

But using technology to increase managerial control only com-plicated Citibank's back-office dilemma. For it misconceived what constituted "efficiency" in this particular work setting. In order to fa-cilitate their insertion into the computerized automation system, the services that the bank provided had to be routinized and simplified. This classic mass-production strategy was reminiscent of Henry Ford's comment about his Model T—a customer could have any color as long as it was black. But in the highly competitive world of international financial services, such a narrow product line was nowhere near good enough. "By imposing a kind of product uniformity on our processing," writes Matteis, "we had sacrificed what is the very essence of a financial transaction service: its uniqueness."

What the Citibank back office really needed, he argued, was a more flexible and adaptable work organization, designed to provide timely and high-quality services rather than just churning out paper products. What if, instead of dividing up the tasks in the back office, they were woven together into a coherent whole? What if, in the letter-of-credit office, for example, each worker handled the *entire* issuing process from start to finish for one customer or a specific set of customers, rather than repeating the same isolated task for them all? And what if technology was used to support this redesign of work, rather than simply freezing the inefficient organization already in place? The idea behind Paradise was to use a new generation of computer technology—minicomputers and distributed data processing—to create a decentralized flexible organization in which a variety of tasks (and, eventually, of services) could be performed by the same worker at a computerized "work station."

Matteis's idea was no soft humanistic experiment in "job enrichment." The ultimate goal was rationalizing the work and reducing the number of people necessary to perform the processing jobs. But the payoff, he argued, was that everyone would benefit. By simplifying and "cleaning up" the work process, the department would require fewer workers and labor costs would plummet. By giving those workers who remained more responsibility in meeting the needs of customers, more training in the new technology, and higher salaries, both worker motivation and quality of work would improve. And by putting together the pieces of the back-office puzzle, jobs would become more skilled, more challenging, and more satisfying than ever before. Paradise, writes Matteis, "would entail making our work force more professional."

But Paradise was to be different not only in the design of the back-office jobs. It was also to pay special attention to the intricacies of "managing change." "How people would respond was of paramount importance," Matteis writes, "and figured in our planning in the earliest stages." In other words, the Citibank managers saw technological change as a social process—not just the introduction of new machines or even new work practices, but the creation of a new work culture where workers would identify with the new technology because it was "an expression of the institution's *raison d'être.*" "The managing of the change is very, very difficult," says one of the managers of the Paradise team. "But one of the things you can always sell is that everybody thinks they're the best. So, you make a big deal about the upgrading and the fact that they're going to be more satisfied in their jobs."

Unlike Steve Taylor and Texas International, managers at Citibank informed workers of the redesign project in advance. While no one would be laid off as a result of the changes, only the very best would be able to stay in the new jobs, they said. The transition would be difficult, they warned; it would take hard work and a great deal of retraining. For those who succeeded, however, the gains would be immense. The new jobs would amount to a substantial upgrade. Managers even coined a new term to describe the new positions: the clerical workers would become "work station professionals."

Despite all this attention to "the human connection," however, Paradise managers were careful to keep the role that workers played in the project within strict limits. For example, no clerical workers were involved in actually determining how the back-office jobs would be redesigned or how technology would be used in them. And while the managers did set up a special experimental environment known as the White Room in which they could study how workers did their jobs and try out new approaches to intregrated processing, the workers' role was entirely passive. They were providing their knowledge of the work process, not making choices about how that knowledge would be used.

The only time office workers were allowed to help shape their new workplace was *after* the jobs had been redesigned and the technical systems developed. A "space-planning" firm was hired to consult with employees on the layout of their new work environment. They helped choose office furniture, color schemes, and the like. "We spent a lot of money on window-dressing," recalls one member of the Paradise management team.

At the same time, Paradise managers worked hard to make sure their scenario for organizational change proceeded smoothly. For them, driving toward "social stability" in the workplace meant maintaining their control over the change process and, when necessary, smothering dissent. "We tried to isolate the nay-sayers," says one team member. And whenever workers tried to disagree or question the scenario that Paradise managers had set out for them, "managing change" immediately reverted to practices suspiciously similar to the legacy of Taylorism. "A lot of people didn't like the process," says Citibank's Matteis. "They insisted on holding on to what we used to call the 'technical mystique.'" What he means is that workers sometimes tried to dissent from management's plans for their work and their skills. "They didn't want to share their knowledge with us," Matteis continues. "They didn't like our taking their technical knowledge and putting it into the system."

One veteran back-office worker, for example, had compiled a special file over the years, outlining the work procedures he had developed in order to perform his job effectively. "He got very upset when we asked for his file. Because, you see, that was taking away his job security." What happened when workers objected to certain aspects of the Paradise plan? "We just continually forced the procedure," says Matteis.

In effect, "user participation" at Citibank was a kind of forced march into the brave new workplace. Not surprisingly, it was enormously stressful for many of the workers involved. Consider the example of what, for Matteis and other Citibank managers, represents the most comprehensive stage of worker participation in the project—the process by which the back-office clerks were trained for their new computerized jobs. Matteis and his team decided to let employees, each of them expert in one narrow aspect of the processing function, to "cross-train" one another. During the day, workers would educate one another in the various facets of the integrated processing job. At night, they would attend classes to learn how to operate the new computer technology. The office was even open on weekends for those who wanted to practice on the new equipment.

However, the entire participatory training process was taking place while the number of jobs in the letter-of-credit department was decreasing—which everyone knew. Simply because of the redesign of the jobs (what Matteis calls the "management control process"), the number of steps in the letter-of-credit issuing process was reduced by half and the workforce in the department cut from 142 to 100 people. By the time the new computer technology was introduced to support this streamlined work organization, the number of workers had been pared to 55. Cross-training thus became a competition for a shrinking number of places. "The most difficult part was that some people were able to cut the mustard and some couldn't," remembers one Paradise line manager. "Some people were geared to change and some were not. The younger people caught on faster than the older people. They were more flexible and went a lot farther." In the early stage of the project, the failure rate in the cross-training program approached 50 percent. "These people are no longer part of our world," says the manager.

But what about the workers who *were* fortunate enough to win the coveted new jobs as work station professionals? Did the promise of better, more satisfying work come true for them? Salaries for the new work station professional jobs rose considerably compared to those of the previous clerical positions. They range from $15,000 to $30,000 per year; some workers were able to double their salary. And with the added responsibility for a complete product and for specific customers, say Paradise managers, workers became more committed to their jobs. In his *Harvard Business Review* article, Matteis makes the characteristic claim: "Gone are the stultifying effects on human energy and motivation often caused by the specialization of labor."

And yet the same ambiguity expressed in the process of technological change at Citibank can be found in the very structure of the new back-office jobs. Being a "professional" implies a certain degree of autonomy and independence. Nevertheless, the back-office workers at 111 Wall Street are subject to the same kind of computerized productivity monitoring that other workers endure in the brave new workplace. "We know what is being done every minute and how it is being done," says one back-office manager. "There is a much more efficient hierarchy of control." "People are more accountable now," says another. "I can pinpoint right away who does something wrong."

Workers are not exactly unaware of this contradiction between "professional" work and computerized control. However, the terms of their "personalized" jobs make it all the more difficult to direct their frustrations at anyone but themselves. "It gets you upset, in a way, because you think these people don't trust you," says one Citibank back-office worker about the monitoring. "If you're really a professional, then they should just give you the responsibility to do your work. If your productivity index is low, well, maybe there's a good reason for it." But instead of reflecting on how little autonomy or control she really has in her job, a few minutes later she has turned the issue from one about management power into one about her own personal capacity. "You have your work and you do it," she continues, "no matter how much you have to do. How you do it is your problem, as long as you get it done. If we are really work station professionals, then we've got to learn how to control ourselves."

For this worker, what is "personalized" in the brave new workplace is control. "We've got to learn to control ourselves." While managers such as Portner or Strassman suggest that this kind of internalized control will replace the traditional mechanisms of bureaucratic management, what is more common is a situation like Citibank's—a combination of the two. The impersonal control of the computer and the personal control of the committed worker ensure that management's traditional authority remains unchallenged.

But there is a world of difference between being allowed to control certain limited areas of working life defined entirely by the norms and decisions of others, and having the influence actually to shape the scope and the content of those norms and decisions themselves. For this reason, the technical consultant who worked at Citibank and observed much of the Paradise project firsthand sees it as an elaborate shadowplay.

"I call it 'the Great Leap Sideways,' " he says. "They wanted to cast a new image for their employees, and in a certain sense they did. They succeeded in creating this atmosphere of change. But what they didn't really change was the organization. There is a fundamental difference between someone who does what he's told and someone who can make decisions. What they still have is 'officers' and 'men.' "

Like Citibank's Paradise project, the human connection is a hybrid, an attempt to elicit worker commitment to managerial plans for work and technology over which they have no control. It offers workers participation, but participation without power. One technology manager compares the human connection to marketing. "Marketing is basically trying to get people to do something that, left to their own devices, they might not do," he told me. "That's exactly what we're trying to do with technology."

And immediately after he tells his story about the machine shop where workers sabotaged the computer, the former IBM systems designer says: "You learn real fast in this business. I used to go in to Mary in the accounting department of some firm and say, 'Mary, why don't you tell me how the work is done here, because we're going to automate it.' Do you think she would tell me? No way! Now, I know enough to say, 'Mary, you are the corporate genius of accounts receivable. How would you use the computer to help you?' You get better answers out of Mary then."

The distance between Steve Taylor and these managers is not great. Their comments suggest that the entire language of the "human connection" is really the opposite of what it first seems. It is not entirely coincidental that terms such as "roleware" and "human factors engineering" and even "user participation" draw upon the technical language of the computer. For they represent not so much the "humanizing" of technology as the "programming" of attitudes, motivations, and human behavior. Even as they personalize work and technology, they reinforce the perception of workers that they are part of the machine.

Authentic participation in the brave new workplace (and genuine "social stability" as well) would require thinking of workers as something more than "users," the performers of certain functions in the work system. It would mean understanding that they bring social interests to work that need to be taken into account. Real participation in technological change would involve seeing the design and use of technology in the workplace as the outcome of a kind of negotiation in which diverse interests and alternative social choices are considered. It would give workers a say in the ends of technological change, instead of limiting their involvement to predetermined questions of means.

However, instead of conceiving of work as a realm of social choice, the managers of the brave new workplace are applying this idea of highly personalized managerial control not only to technology but to the corporation itself. They are making the reenchantment of the workplace into an organizing principle for all working life.

CHAPTER FIVE

CRAFTING THE CORPORATE SELF

As TRADITIONAL BUREAUCRATIC METHODS for shaping what Weber called the "psycho-physical apparatus of man" prove increasingly ineffective, the managers of the brave new workplace are beginning to define a new set of managerial tools. As they do, the reenchantment of the workplace is spreading from technology to the corporation itself.

One sign of this phenomenon is the proliferation of new approaches to corporate management during the past decade. Formal company programs such as quality circles, employee participation teams, quality of work life projects, and the like are expanding throughout industry (according to a survey by the New York Stock Exchange, they currently exist at some 14 percent of American companies with 100 employees or more). Popular new approaches based on "Theory Z," "corporate culture," and the managerial secrets of the Japanese have captured the imagination not only of the business community but of society as a whole. The motivations of these diverse initiatives are many; the forms they take are legion. But they all seem to be part of a more general trend: to meet the crisis of scientific management by concentrating on worker motivation and morale and, in this way, win employee commitment to and participation in the corporation's goals for working life. "A powerful movement is underway," *Fortune* magazine has announced, "to reexamine and, as necessary, break with old managerial assumptions [and] the rigidity and formalism of the past. If it isn't entirely a leap into the unknown, it nonetheless leads into a wilderness of human emotions and power relationships."

Although few managers would put it quite that way, the *Fortune* metaphor is exactly right. For whatever else this growing preoccupation with new management styles and techniques may represent, it also signifies a foray of modern management into the murky emotions of working life. Just as scientific management adjusted individuals to the demands of bureaucratic organization and the Taylorized factory, these new tools of management seek to adjust the contemporary worker to the unique demands of the brave new workplace. And as befits the nature of "abstract" work, they are primarily psychological and symbolic in nature—designed to manage the values people bring to work and the meanings they find in it, as well as work itself.

This trend envisions an enchanted corporation, whose model is not Weber's smooth-functioning machine but a community of shared values and shared feelings. In that persistent cliché, it is a "family" that speaks to the desire for meaningful work. What this enchanted corporation offers is not merely narrow work roles but a social identity, not merely a job but a new "corporate self."

Seen against the backdrop of authoritarian managerial control—the kind that produces the frustration of Dave Boggs, the disillusion of Diana Osborne, the anxiety of Elaine Jensen—this may sound enormously appealing. For it seems to provide a way to humanize not just technology but the entire corporation, to bring work back under human control. However, just as the claims of scientific management lend themselves to social domination, so too does this emerging sensibility of the enchanted corporation.

When managerial control becomes "personalized," the relationship of workers to the corporation is understood in exclusively psychological and individual terms. The very idea of power and control becomes purely therapeutic, a matter of feeling rather than action. And the genuine conflicts of working life—and, indeed, of all social life—themselves become personalized, dismissed as matters of mere individual preference or, worse, social deviance, rather than recognized as legitimate subjects of social and political choice.

Thus, the reenchantment of the workplace constitutes the culmination of corporate control over work rather than an alternative to it. Instead of disappearing behind the seemingly rational impersonal rules of bureaucracy or the automatic imperatives of technological change, this time the complex play of power in the workplace vanishes behind the mask of this corporate self. And when the very purpose of corporate management becomes the harnessing of human values and emotions to the ends of corporate competitiveness and market success, the result is the antithesis of the humanization of work. It is the ultimate rationalization of the brave new workplace: not merely the rationalization of work and technology but the rationalization of the human personality as well.

To grasp the logic of this reenchantment of work, a useful starting point is a recent book with an evocative title: *The Leader: A New Face for American Management.* Its author is Dr. Michael Maccoby, director of Harvard University's Program on Work, Technology, and Character and "quality of work life" consultant to corporations and unions. He sees the crisis of modern management as a kind of psychological drama, and his book sketches the outlines of a corporate response.

According to Maccoby, the very triumph of instrumental rationality in the workplace, first signaled by Weber, has produced its opposite: the development of a qualitatively new "social character" in American society which undermines the effectiveness of bureaucratic management. Like the proponents of the human connection, Maccoby assigns rapid technological change a major role in this process. The spread of new technologies, he writes, is demanding "new adaptive traits and abilities" from people, in particular "an openness to new ideas."

But equally important has been the establishment of the corporation as the dominant institution in American society. For this has brought about a corresponding decline of social identity based on small, local communities. Increasingly, "individuals are raised to be flexible and mobile," writes Maccoby. "Relationships are not provided by place and family; they must be created and developed." This loosening of traditional bonds, brought about by technology and bureaucracy, has led to what Maccoby calls a "challenge to paternal authority" across the spectrum of American institutional life—and nowhere more profoundly than in the workplace itself.

Together, these changes have produced a social character whose highest value is the conscious construction of a "self." In a world where technological change is radically transforming traditional occupational subcultures, where geographical communities no longer root people in time and place, and where traditional authorities and conventional wisdoms are constantly questioned, the texture of personal identity grows thin, its outlines blurred. And the task of building a coherent self becomes a compelling project—indeed, a necessity. Thus, the new social character is "more oriented to self than to craft, enterprise, or career," Maccoby writes. And the self becomes a strategy, a tool (at one point, Maccoby even calls it a "fine-tuned instrument") to be deployed in the service of "personal growth."

Where Weber saw "disenchantment" as the unfortunate yet inevitable accompaniment of bureaucracy's triumph, Maccoby claims it sounds a death knell for bureaucracy itself. The search for self-fulfillment that disenchantment eventually engenders does not mix well with the demands of bureaucratic control. As Maccoby writes, "People oriented to self-expression will resent submission to such authority." And as a new generation of workers moves into the American workplace, corporations are running the risk of actually stimulating the "negative" side of the new social character: a "passive and unproductive adaptation to new organization and technology"; "alienation, detachment, and disloyalty"; "undisciplined self-indulgence ... which one rationalizes as self-fulfillment"; and, most dangerous of all in the brave new workplace where new technologies impose new responsibilities on the workforce, "cynical rebelliousness."

Maccoby's book poses the question: how to manage this new social character? The answer is for the corporation to embrace this search for a self and harness the new social character to its own ends. If modern management can be imbued with a "self-development ethic" all its own, if workers can be made to see the corporation as the pathway not only to financial security but to personal growth and psychological identity, then the negatives of the new social character will be turned into positives. And the alienation and disloyalty experienced by workers in the bureaucratic corporation will be replaced by intense personal commitment to and total involvement in working life. As Maccoby puts it, "Properly organized, workers can manage themselves."

Maccoby's prognosis has echoes of the "social stability" that Paul Strassman imagines. And, like Strassman, he sets his image of a corporation dedicated to "self-development" in opposition to the authoritarian management that still holds sway in many American workplaces. And yet, there is something that rings false in this contrast, something too simple and too neat. For one thing, when Maccoby talks about this new self as a "fine-tuned instrument," the echo is not of Strassman but of Weber's description of bureaucracy itself. It is almost as if he is inadvertently suggesting not the transcendence of instrumental rationality but its extension into the realm of the human personality. And when Maccoby analyzes the changes transforming the American workplace, especially those having to do with technological change, his psychological categories reduce what are genuine struggles over power and control (struggles about technology, skills, work organization, and the like) to mere "negative" character traits, personality flaws rather than political conflicts of interest. For Maccoby, the conflicts over control in the brave new workplace appear somehow adolescent or anachronistic—they are "undisciplined," "self-indulgent," even "cynical." But this opens the door to a dangerous phenomenon that truly deserves to be called cynical—the systematic manipulation by corporate managers of people's desire for meaningful work.

That this reenchantment of the workplace is especially susceptible to manipulation is patently clear in another recent—and enormously popular—book. Where Maccoby provides a rationale for reenchantment, its authors suggest the techniques for managing this new corporate self. Their particular version of the enchanted corporation has become so fashionable that it was the best-selling nonfiction book of 1983. Thomas Peters and Robert Waterman's *In Search of Excellence* (based on the findings of their "excellent companies" survey, conducted at the prominent management consulting firm McKinsey and Company, and distilling the lessons they have gleaned from some sixty of America's "best-run" companies) promises nothing less than a new rationality of corporate life.

For Peters and Waterman, the key to making the corporation a source of fulfillment and identity for its members is to reconceive the job of management as one of "making meaning." "We desperately need meaning in our lives," they write, "and will sacrifice a great deal to the institutions that will provide [it] for us." Peters and Waterman's excellent companies provide meaning and a sense of identity by paying "explicit attention . . . to values" at work. *In Search of Excellence* is designed as a primer to teach corporate managers "just what values ought to be shaped and managed."

Peters and Waterman use various terms to describe this conscious attention to corporate values. The excellent companies provide a "shared culture"; they offer employees "guiding beliefs," "superordinate goals," "transforming purpose," even "faith." If, at times, the authors' idea sounds vaguely religious, it is because Peters and Waterman seem to believe that, in a sense, it is. "Perhaps transcendence is too grand a term for the business world," they write at one point. Nevertheless, the ambience of the excellent companies "comes close to meriting it."

For this reason, the shared values of the excellent companies are not communicated through the formal standards, "calculable rules," and well-defined hierarchical controls of the typical bureaucracy. Again, almost like a religion, they are intimated through stories, rituals, and myths. The excellent companies are "rich tapestries of anecdote, myth, and fairy tale," the authors write. Their members invariably turn to "story, slogan, and legend" in order to express "the characteristics of their own great institutions." These slogans and legends may seem mundane or even silly to the outsider (at one point, Peters and Waterman label them "blatant hoopla and rah-rah"). But, no matter how corny, their constant repetition becomes a wellspring of motivation and commitment. For, in the words of the psychologist Ernest Becker (quoted approvingly by Peters and Waterman), "Ritual is the technique for giving life."

And, like Maccoby, Peters and Waterman see the role of the corporate manager as that of a "transforming leader." In effect, they want to turn Weber on his head and reintroduce the idea of "charisma" into corporate management. No longer the impartial and impersonal expert, the manager is the "value shaper," the "maker of meanings." He is the embodiment of the corporation's unique culture; he fuses the individual to something greater than himself, the institution of the corporation. "By offering meaning as well as money," Peters and Waterman write, "they give their employees a mission as well as a sense of feeling great."

The "transcendence" that Peters and Waterman are talking about is, finally, not metaphysical but psychological—a matter of feeling, a conviction of control. Indeed, the managers of the excellent companies "give people control over their destinies. . . . They turn the average Joe and the average Jane into winners. They let, even insist that, people stick out." And, in the process, they "unleash excitement."

It is an emotionally charged image—more sexual than religious. At another point, the authors say that the excellent companies create "the magic of the turned-on workforce." They produce "charged-up people" who are "excited participants" in business and society as a whole. Elsewhere, they draw on the language of family life to describe this emotional energy. The excellent companies treat employees like "members of the family," and "like good parents, they care . . . a lot—and expect . . . a lot." And they quote a corporate executive who believes that "companies . . . have become sort of a community center for employees, as opposed to just a place to work. . . . With the breakdown of traditional structures . . . companies have filled the void. They have become . . . mother institutions."

Whether the particular image implies sexual excitement or maternal love, the message is the same. The promise of the enchanted corporation is that work will become a "meaningful relationship." And work organizations will elicit the kind of energy and engagement characteristic of highly charged emotional life. The mechanism is to make work *intimate,* to permeate it with an internal "economy of the emotions." In this way, the enchanted corporation will simultaneously make work more fulfilling for the worker and make the worker more suited to the demands of the brave new workplace than the external economy of time and motion reflected in scientific management ever could.

But there is an empty space at the very center of this vision of corporate intimacy and meaning. When it comes to specifying precisely *what* values the corporation should encourage, Peters and

Waterman are remarkably vague. At one point, they repeat the buzzwords of some of their excellent companies along with the relativistic assurance that while such slogans may sound superficial, "[these] values are transforming for the companies that live them." At another, they remark that "form precedes substance," as if to suggest that the content of any firm's values is far less important than the mere fact of having some (or any). And they end their book with the ethically empty comment of a corporate executive who wanted his employees to be "the best" at something—"he doesn't really care much what."

Perhaps the least equivocal description of what Peters and Waterman really mean by "shared values" comes not in their book but in an earlier article based upon their research at McKinsey. Here they talk about "superordinate goals" being "like the postulates in a mathematical system. They are the starting points on which the system is logically built, but in themselves are not logically derived." If superordinate goals or shared values are "postulates" with no logical justification, then what *is* their rationale? "The ultimate test of their value is not their logic but the usefulness of the system that ensues."

But "usefulness" defined by what and by whom? "Usefulness" to what end? Peters and Waterman would probably respond by saying something like "success in the marketplace." But this is a concept of value as narrowly utilitarian and relentlessly instrumental as that of any bureaucratic system. One might even say that where Weber defined an "instrumental rationality," Peters and Waterman offer an "instrumental irrationality" in which self-development, culture, and personal identity all become subordinated to the corporation's control over work. And while the form may be different from that of a traditional bureaucracy, the ends are identical. Thus, Peters and Waterman inform us that their excellent companies are as "tough" and as "measurement-happy" as any traditional work organization. Only the mechanism is less the external measures of Taylorism than internalized attitudes and constant peer pressure. While "this is not control via massive forms and incalculable numbers and variables," they assure us that "it is the toughest control of all."

Not surprisingly, many of the young managers in the brave new workplace who have embraced this new managerial sensibility understand both "values" and the people they are managing in precisely the same narrow instrumental way.

One revealing example is a conversation I had with a student at the Harvard Business School and an enthusiastic participant in something called the Human Resources Management Club. When it came to describing her own management philosophy, she turned to the same highly personalized and frankly sexual metaphors that Peters and Waterman and other spokespersons for the reenchantment of the workplace use. The ultimate challenge for the manager in the brave new workplace, she told me, is "to figure out what your employee's hot-button is."

By way of explanation, she related a story from her own brief but promising management career. Appropriately enough, it concerns the familiar issue of workplace technological change. Before she came to Harvard, she had been in charge of the automation of a foreign exchange office at a major New York bank. Most of the workers in the office were women; many were black or Hispanic, many were part-timers from local high schools. In the beginning, she remembers, the bank employees were dubious. "I was Ivy League and college-educated," she says, "and their attitude was, 'Here is the whiz kid, coming in and taking over, thinks she can change the world.'" The workers were hesitant to cooperate; they didn't see what was in it for them. "They would give me incorrect information about their work, things like that."

So she set out to win their "trust." "I started having a lot of meetings to get them to feel more relaxed about automation," she explains. "They were very concerned, so I was sort of preparing them for the change. You don't want them to feel that they don't have control of their jobs anymore. I wanted to make them feel that they had a little input into the decisions." There was only one problem: "Of course, they really didn't," she continues, without missing a beat. "There was a management task force for that. So it was sort of window dressing."

For this manager, the distinction between *feeling* in control and actually *being* in control might as well be nonexistent. For her, the purpose of the new management style is merely therapeutic, to nurture those worker attitudes and feelings "useful" to the smooth functioning of the work organization (as defined by management) without actually providing them with any real influence over managerial choices and decisions.

"People like to feel in control," she continues. "So, let them feel in control." The participatory manager cannot "strut around and say, 'I've got the power.'" But, then again, he or she "can't be their best friend or become their equal either. You always have to recognize that you *do* have the power. It's just how you demonstrate it."

Sometimes, she admits, the fit between intimate work and unequal power can cause delicate problems. "You become a lot closer to people," she says, "and then it's a lot harder to fire them when you have to." And yet, even then, her model for dealing with such difficulties remains that of the intimate personal relationship. The old authoritarian approach "is like going out with someone and then all of a sudden, breaking off without ever telling them why. When you fire somebody, they should know they're going to be fired. They should know why." In any love relationship, it's the least one would expect. But it never seems to cross this manager's mind that a work relationship is different, not exactly reciprocal; that while she has the power to "break up" with her employee, the employee does not have the power to break up with her—short of leaving the workplace altogether.

As a result, her approach to management becomes an elaborate manipulation. Let people feel in control without actually giving up your own power. Provide them with a pretense of participation in decisions that in fact are beyond their influence and control. Elicit the energy and engagement of close personal relationships, but make sure those relationships always remain contingent on "usefulness" and performance. And don't ever become so close or committed to any particular relationship, any particular person, that it becomes an obstacle to exercising your authority.

This is the heart of the sensibility of the enchanted corporation. Indeed, Peters and Waterman even have a name for it. They call it the "illusion of control." "If people think they have even modest personal control over their destinies," they write, "they will persist at tasks. They will do better at them. They will become more committed to them. . . . The fact . . . that we *think* we have a *bit* more discretion leads to *much* greater commitment." In the survey materials from McKinsey and Company on which *In Search of Excellence* is based, they add that this "drive for perceived control" is "one of a tiny handful of fundamental motivations" to be managed by the "conscious creation of institutional cultures."

But there is a difference between "perceived control" and the real thing. In the interstices between the two, the enchanted corporation is creating new forms of social domination and the potential for serious abuse.

There is a moment in *In Search of Excellence* when the authors interrupt their celebration of the enchanted corporation in order to admit the existence of a dark cloud on the otherwise shining horizon. "For us, the most worrisome part of a strong culture," Peters and Waterman write, "is the ever present possibility of abuse." When managerial authority becomes intimate, it speaks to some of our deepest needs for security. "Unfortunately, in seeking security, most people seem all too willing to yield to authority, and, in providing meaning through rigidly held beliefs, others are all too willing to exert power."

As if to underline just how dangerous this tendency can be, Peters and Waterman go on to recount the well-known story of Yale psychologist Stanley Milgram's experiments on obedience. In a researchlike setting, a "white-coated experimenter" gave a test to an individual strapped to a chair. Milgram's subjects were directed by the experimenter to administer electric shocks to the individual whenever he gave an incorrect answer. Unbeknownst to the subjects, the "shocks" they were delivering were bogus, and the victim receiving them was a trained actor. What Milgram discovered was that the vast majority of his subjects accepted the authority of the experiment leader without question, even when it meant forcing the "victim" to endure what appeared to be excruciating pain. Milgram concluded that American culture "had failed almost entirely in inculcating internal controls on actions having their origins in authority."

The subjects of Milgram's experiments may have been "excited participants," but certainly not in the way that Peters and Waterman have in mind. However, they raise this "possibility of abuse" only to dismiss it. Fortunately, the excellent companies have a "saving grace." They are not "inwardly focused." Their ever-present relationships with their customers inject a "sense of balance and proportion into an otherwise possibly claustrophobic environment." Once again, the marketplace solves all problems.

But the dynamic of power in the enchanted corporation is nowhere near so simple. The possibility of abuse, far from being the occasional by-product of power-hungry managers or overly submissive subordinates, is built into the very logic of intimate authority. Despite all the emphasis on "participation" and "commitment," the reenchantment of the workplace leaves workers with a curiously passive role. They have little ability actually to determine what the values or priorities of a particular corporation will be. For Peters and Waterman, they are left with only one narrow choice: either "buying into" the corporate culture or "opting out." "There's no halfway house for most people in the excellent companies," they write. "You either buy into their norms or get out." And even when workers are encouraged to participate in certain aspects of managerial decision-making, their participation is invariably limited and circumscribed. When they try to step out of their narrow role, the illusion of control is quickly transformed into the reality of its absence.

No workplace comes closer to embodying the vision of the enchanted corporation than the birthplace of the new computer technology—the research labs and assembly plants of California's Silicon Valley. The lush amenities of the high-tech workplace (including recreation centers and swimming pools), the easy informal atmosphere marked by the absence of executive parking spaces, dining rooms, office suites, even suits and ties, the picnics and barbecues and Friday-afternoon "beer busts," the profusion of innovative management programs ranging from flextime, job rotation, and autonomous work groups to employee stock options, paid educational leaves, and even university-style sabbaticals have all become familiar signposts of a distinctive corporate ethic and identity.

When one asks Silicon Valley managers about their high-tech management style, they tend to explain it as a response to the managerial challenges of the brave new workplace. They point to the pressures created by the Valley's volatile economic environment characterized by rapid growth, intense competition, and high employee turnover. "We have the closest thing to a true free-market environment out here," says Bruce Noel, a manager for new business planning and development at the ROLM Corporation, the fast-growing Santa Clara, California, manufacturer of advanced telecommunications equipment (and, since November 1984, wholly owned subsidiary of IBM). "You have a real problem building loyalty. When you are driving people that hard you need an outlet."

They also emphasize the special problems that come with managing the new workers of the young generation that make up a large portion of the Valley's electronics industry workforce. "People in general are more into personal development," says a member of the ROLM personnel department. "At the lower end of the pay scale, they aren't so demanding about the work you give them, but they want to be treated right." Echoing Maccoby, she describes the typical attitude this way: " 'I need to self-actualize, and if I don't get real job satisfaction here, I'll go somewhere else.' " Given the opportunities for mobility among the Valley's many high-technology firms, "any intelligent business man or woman is going to try to respond to that," she says. "You're not going to be competitive if you don't."

Finally Silicon Valley managers always return to the unique demands of state-of-the-art computer technology itself. In an industry where innovation is a daily imperative, where the typical product life cycle is a scant two or three years, and where highly trained scientific and technical personnel make up nearly 40 percent of the workforce and are the key to any firm's success, the motivation and commitment of employees becomes an economic necessity. "When people are working in highly specialized jobs, where nobody knows the whole answer, you can't be autocratic and hierarchical," says a director of organizational development at Signetics, one of the Valley's leading semiconductor manufacturers. "You have to have participation, people need to be in a position to manage and control their own work."

The volatile economic environment, the new values of a predominantly young workforce, the breakneck pace of technological innovation itself are like so many centrifugal forces threatening to pull the corporation apart. In order to counteract these destabilizing tendencies, Silicon Valley firms weave a cocoon of institutional attachments around work stretching from the top to the bottom of the corporation.

"The ROLMs and Hewlett-Packards provide a more total environment for people," explains ROLM's Bruce Noel. Whether by means of recreation centers or management practices emphasizing teamwork or even highly visible "hoopla and rah-rah" at company social events, the goal is always the same: "to attach people to the work environment," say Noel, "to involve them so that they feel part of the business."

Noel gives the example of employee stock options. On the one hand, they are a mechanism allowing start-up companies to keep wages down when the firm is small and capital is scarce. But stock options serve a much broader and more intangible function. They tie the individual's financial status to the actual performance of the firm. They symbolize the bond between worker and company. "They lock people in," says Noel. "They're a financial lock."

Even the occasional beer bust can serve this fundamental goal. To the outsider, it may appear to be little more than a trivial social occasion. But for Bruce Noel, it is a kind of ritual, an apprenticeship in corporate loyalty and belonging. At a ROLM beer bust, says Noel, "everyone doesn't just sit around drinking beer." Managers give talks on last quarter's earnings or the latest challenge from the Japanese competition. They explain how a particular product line fits into the company's overall strategic plan. The beer bust becomes an arena of corporate communication, a way to "have everyone know where things are going"—and not only top-level managers like Noel but "all the way to little Suzy down there, stuffing the printed circuit board. She gets information on what the product is for. She has an idea of the whole board."

It is a striking image. Little Suzy may be down there on the assembly line working at a somewhat narrow and in itself perhaps even uninteresting job. Nevertheless, she is able to transcend the limits of that job and become linked to the purpose of the corporation as a whole. She is not only "locked in financially" but, says Noel, "locked in mentally." And in return for her devotion and commitment, for her energy and attention, she receives the self-actualization that the personnel manager describes. "We build identity," says Noel, "and a sense of common direction."

A Silicon Valley management consultant puts it this way: "Work should be an extension of who you are as a human being. That should be part of the goals of any company. We want the worker to be out in the kitchen dealing with all the heat, but what are we going to do for him besides giving him some money? Well, maybe we had better take care of his psyche as well."

Taking care of the psyche is the end point of the reenchantment of the workplace. And yet there is one aspect of work in Silicon Valley's high-technology electronics industry that these managers only hint at. When they talk vaguely about workers "at the lower end of the pay scale" or imagine, rather condescendingly, "little Suzy down there, stuffing the printed circuit board," they are referring to the fact that, despite Silicon Valley's ethic of corporate loyalty and community, its high-tech workforce is economically and sociologically among the most *divided* in American industry today.

While it is true that high-paid engineers and computer scientists make up nearly half of the electronics industry workforce, the other half consists of low-wage production workers. They tend the continuous-process machinery used in the fabrication of silicon chips; they put together integrated circuits by attaching fine metal wires to the chips under high-powered microscopes; like "little Suzy," they stuff the circuits into printed circuit boards used in the assembly of whole computer systems; and they test electronic products, calibrate equipment, and maintain the machinery used throughout the electronics production process. Their experience of Silicon Valley is so different from that of the engineers that it is as if they work in an entirely different industry.

Wages constitute the most dramatic evidence of this divide. High-tech industry has made California's Santa Clara County one of the most affluent communities in the nation with an average annual wage of more than $28,500 in 1983 (compared to the national average of $17,544). And yet, high tech production workers make on average 30 percent less than workers in other manufacturing industries, a gap exacerbated by the high cost of living in Silicon Valley.

Over a decade ago, in 1972, the average engineering technician in the Valley earned 80 percent more than the average production worker. Between 1974 and 1978, the average salary for the inexperienced engineer increased 33 percent, but that of the entry-level assembler grew only 7 percent. By 1981, salaries for starting engineers with a B.A. degree in electronics were averaging about $22,500; Ph.D. engineers were earning $33,500. And chief engineers were commanding as much as $72,000 to $90,000. However, in 1985, entry-level semiconductor production workers are still earning as little as $4.50 an hour (those with two to four year's experience make between $6 and $8 an hour). And for those people working at the small shops which supply printed circuit boards and other components to the major manufacturers, pay-rates are often little higher than the minimum wage.

The divide is also evident in who makes up Silicon Valley's two workforces. High-tech firms draw on a world market of top educational and technical talent for technical and professional jobs; a surprisingly large portion of the Valley's engineers are foreign-born. Production work, however, remains the preserve of women and ethnic minorities. Noel's example of "little Suzy" is sociologically accurate. While women constitute 40 percent of the total electronics workforce in Silicon Valley, they make up 75 percent of the assemblers and 65 percent of the operatives. As employment in the industry has boomed, women workers have been supplemented by various ethnic minorities (in particular, Hispanics) as well as new immigrant groups such as Filipinos and Vietnamese. About 60 percent of assemblers are members of minority groups.

Finally, the mobility between high-tech firms is rarely matched by mobility within firms. There are few avenues for advancement from one side of the Silicon Valley divide to the other. The rapid growth of some firms has created opportunities for production workers to move into certain middle-level technical jobs. The expansion of sales, marketing, and personnel staffs has opened other possibilities for women working in clerical jobs. But the educational qualifications necessary for the most interesting and challenging technical jobs in the industry constitute a major obstacle to upward mobility from the production workforce to the ranks of technical and engineering personnel.

What does the existence of this sharply divided workforce mean for Silicon Valley's distinctive management style? It could be that of all the centrifugal forces to which high-tech managers must attend, this is the most important. In a workforce so evenly divided down the middle, an image of the corporation as a "community" may be all the more essential. And yet, precisely because of this division, the low-wage workers of Silicon Valley's production and clerical workforce often experience this community differently than their managers do. For them, the "total environment" of the enchanted corporation can become a burden.

Someone I shall call Lisa Morgan comes close to Bruce Noel's imaginary "little Suzy" of Silicon Valley. A twenty-six-year-old clerical worker, she makes about $12,000 a year working at perhaps one of the most famous of Silicon Valley's high-technology corporations (and one of the best-known of Peters and Waterman's "excellent companies")—the computer and instruments manufacturer Hewlett-Packard. Five years ago, Morgan came to her new job at HP full of excitement and expectation; she had heard that the company was "a really humane place to work." Over the years, however, her opinion has changed dramatically. She has learned that when the corporation takes care of the psyche, "there is always a price."

Morgan is a member of Hewlett-Packard's customer service and sales organization. She spends her day typing airway bills and sending telexes to customers through the company's worldwide "Heart" computer system. She describes her job as "very clerical, very boring." "Everything is departmentalized. You're just reduced to being functional. It's like Henry Ford and the assembly line."

Like others in the brave new workplace, Morgan's performance is monitored by the computer system she works on. "Virtually everything I do requires plugging into the computer," she says. "I'm number 1602 and if 1602 makes a mistake, a report—like a little report card—spits out what my mistake was and how much it cost in transmission time, that type of thing. When you do make an error on the system, it has to go through your boss before you can see it. There is no opportunity to correct what you did wrong."

However, there is one major difference between Morgan's job and, say, that of an AT&T operator. Although her job is rather narrow and limited, the commitment to it that the company demands is total. "I thought that if I just did my job, it would be enough," Morgan reflects. "I found out that it's not. They are constantly telling you how important you are to the company. You would think that what I'm doing would shut them down in a minute—if I took a vacation or something. They try to make you feel that. They want you to be the person who shows up on Saturday and Sunday and who works until eleven o'clock at night—and not just once in a while but constantly. They demand so much from . . . from your *life*!"

For Morgan, the elaborate mechanisms to attach workers to the work environment in Silicon Valley are really techniques of intrusiveness, designed to enforce not just efficient work performance but a specific kind of social behavior. In her department, no one exactly said so, but it soon became clear that workday social events were mandatory—"a way to see you in a different situation," she says. When, at one point, she stopped going to HP's fabled morning coffee break, her supervisor told her that "Bill and Dave"—the by now quasi-legendary founders of Hewlett-Packard—"give you this ten minutes and you really ought to take advantage of it." One time, a manager even chided her for not smiling enough. She was a representative of Hewlett-Packard wherever she went, Morgan was informed. Looking gloomy was a bad reflection on the company.

Such examples may sound trivial, but they are important because they indicate that when personality becomes a function of the corporation, intimate work becomes unrelentingly public work. Take the example of Hewlett-Packard's famous "open office." It is regularly described as an effective means to break down the formality and status-conscious hierarchies of traditional firms. According to Lisa Morgan, who has worked in one, the open office has the added effect of making it virtually impossible to have any privacy at work. "All the managers are strategically located," she says, "so that *everything* is seen: who is talking to his or her neighbor, who is on the telephone—maybe it isn't a business call—who is late and trying to get in through the warehouse, things like that. There is no privacy whatsoever. It's impossible to have a confidential conversation."

Then there is the company's "open door" policy, in which workers have the right to go over their immediate supervisor's head and take complaints to higher levels of management. In Morgan's department, the policy became a victim of the fundamental ambiguity in authority relationships in the enchanted corporation. "They're trying to be your chums," she says about HP managers. "You have to be very careful. One minute, they sound interested and constructive; the next, you learn that what you have said has gotten back to someone else." As a result, "anything you have to say is pretty much public knowledge. Everyone knows."

At its worst, the intrusiveness of the enchanted corporation can become a kind of coercion, founded on peer pressure and the practice of public humiliation. In her years at Hewlett-Packard, Morgan has seen supervisors publicly criticize individual employees' performances, discuss the possibility of firing one employee in front of others, even announce the dismissal of someone in front of a divisional assembly—"just to let you know that we do fire people sometimes at HP." (Fortunately for the person involved, she was informed of her dismissal beforehand; she did not have to witness her public expulsion from the enchanted corporation.) The accumulation of such incidents makes the corporation a nearly constant presence in people's lives. "I always feel the presence of HP," says Morgan. "It's there. And I always, always feel it."

The very mechanisms designed to encourage worker participation also become instruments of social conformity at work. When Morgan's "quality circle" tried to address the problem of lack of privacy in their office, the area manager informed them that they were "beyond the scope" of the quality circle process. In such an environment, people who veer from the narrow paths of behavior sanctioned by the corporate culture are left not with self-development but self-doubt and a paralyzing passivity. For to the degree that workers internalize the values of the corporate culture, they tend to blame themselves for its contradictions. Morgan's first response to her growing dissatisfactions with her job was to wonder, "How can

54,000 people be wrong? Maybe it's me. When you're in that kind of position, under that kind of pressure and stress, you really start to think, You know, these guys may be right. Maybe I *am* lucky to be here. I ought to just cool it. Because maybe no one else will want me."

For Lisa Morgan, the reenchantment of the workplace does not resolve the contradictions of control in the brave new workplace. Indeed, it makes them more acute than ever. She dissents from the "self" that the enchanted corporation imposes upon her, but in the absence of other mediating institutions in the workplace she ends up feeling she has nowhere else to turn. Peters and Waterman might wonder why Morgan doesn't simply "opt out," seek her fortune elsewhere, find a corporate culture more amenable to her preferences. But that assumes the same narrowly psychological conception of work implicit in the language of reenchantment. It puts the onus on the individual rather than the institution.

What's more, the abuses of power in the enchanted corporation extend beyond the individual. They can span entire industries and affect whole communities. When they do, the conflicts of the brave new workplace start to break out into the open. And workers begin to question and even to challenge, not themselves, but the ideology of reenchantment itself.

CHAPTER SIX

HAZARDS OF ENCHANTMENT

THE RASH CAN BREAK OUT AT ANY TIME: when she walks down the aisle in the grocery store that holds the laundry detergents and soaps; when she puts on a pair of pants fastened with a metal clasp. In the eight years since she became aware of her allergic reactions, fifty-four-year-old Adele Perez has learned how to bake her own bread (the preservatives in the store-bought kind trigger the rash), to make her own mustard and ketchup (she is allergic to vinegar), and to avoid synthetic clothing and wear only natural fibers. She is also allergic to perfume, tobacco, certain metals, chloride, Teflon, even toothpaste. "My doctor," she tells me, "says I'm allergic to the twentieth century."

Adele Perez suffers from what some doctors call "chemical sensitization," a pronounced tendency to acquire allergies that is brought on by chronic exposure to toxic chemicals. During the twelve years that she worked as an assembler at Varian Associates, a Palo Alto, California, manufacturer of scientific instruments, she was regularly exposed to some twenty-five different chemicals ranging from organic solvents like xylene and freon to acids, epoxies, and metal fumes. Perez stopped working at Varian in 1976. She is so thoroughly "sensitized" that she can no longer work in the electronics industry.

Just as in the coal mines of Appalachia and the textile mills of North Carolina, the steel mills of Pittsburgh and the auto plants of Detroit, work in Silicon Valley's electronics industry can be dangerous to people's health. The health hazards facing high-tech workers—their causes, their symptoms, their long-term effects—are complex and controversial. Medical and industrial health and safety experts still do not know all there is to know about them. Nevertheless, an issue that for years went unrecognized and unacknowledged has recently become the focus of widening public concern: the possibility that occupational health and safety constitute a social problem of heretofore unimagined proportions in the electronics industry.

But the story of Adele Perez and others like her is important for another reason as well. Few issues reveal more vividly the clash of conflicting interests in the workplace than occupational safety and health. In few cases are workers' needs more basic or their lack of control more dangerous. In few situations is it easier for the corporation to ignore long-term problems in favor of its own short-term financial interests. Thus, how Valley firms have chosen to respond to this issue should help us weigh the promises of the reenchantment of the workplace.

The results are far from encouraging. Despite its promise of participation and community, Silicon Valley's high-tech industry has for the most part chosen to protect its own power and interests. Valley firms have hidden behind the utopian image of the charmed corporate community rather than face the growing evidence of a serious health problem. And this has made it all the more difficult for workers and the public to recognize the hazards they face, to protect themselves from them, or even to gain compensation when they become sick. In this respect, the story of Silicon Valley's health hazards probably represents the most systematic failure of corporate responsibility in the brave new workplace today.

A crucial component of Silicon Valley's futuristic image has been the idea that electronics, unlike more traditional manufacturing industries, is clean and pollution-free. The dramatic absence of ugly smokestacks protruding into the sky, the beautifully landscaped grounds and architecturally distinguished buildings, the white smocks and headgear worn by workers in carefully controlled "clean rooms" (where dust levels are rigorously controlled in order to avoid the contamination of silicon chips by impurities)—all contributed to this dominant impression. "It's a high-quality workplace," says Dan Cook of the American Electronics Association in Palo Alto. "You're not going to come home covered with dirt and grease and God knows what else."

At first glance, official health and safety statistics seem to bear out this image. For example, 1982 figures from the federal government's Bureau of Labor Statistics rated the semiconductor industry as the third-safest among some two hundred durable-goods-manufacturing industries. But when data concerning occupational illness are separated out from statistics for one-time injuries, a far more disturbing picture emerges. In 1983 (the most recent available statistics), occupational illnesses in the California semiconductor industry occurred at three times the average rate of illness in general manufacturing industries. They constituted nearly one-quarter of all "work-loss" cases (where employees miss work as a result of occupational illness or injury) in the industry, again three times the average rate for manufacturing as a whole. Nearly half of these cases (41.6 percent in 1983) were caused by exposure to toxic chemicals—what in the language of occupational health and safety experts is known as "systemic poisoning." These systemic poisoning cases accounted for almost 10 percent of all work-loss cases in the semiconductor industry, ten times the rate for manufacturing as a whole. The only industry with a higher level of systemic poisoning was "agricultural chemicals," which includes the manufacturers of highly toxic pesticides.

While most people think of electronics as a close cousin to the electrical equipment industry, the more accurate analogy, as far as health and safety are concerned, is petrochemicals. Toxic chemicals and gases are used at every step of the semiconductor manufacturing process. When silicon crystals are formed, workers add arsenic, phosphorus, and boron to liquid silicon in order to enhance its electrical conductivity. After the crystals are cut into razor-thin wafers, the wafers are cleaned in sulfuric and nitric acid and a variety of solvents, coated in "photoresist" (a light-sensitive material dissolved in solvent), and etched in hydrofluoric acid. Some of the most dangerous poison gases in industry today—arsine, phosphine, and diborane—are used as "dopants" in the diffusion process that creates the transistors on the surface of the chip. Finally, epoxies and metals are used in the bonding, soldering, and electroplating processes. A 1980 study by the California Department of Industrial Relations revealed that in the previous year, some forty-two Silicon Valley semiconductor companies used more than 500,000 gallons of solvents, 2 million gallons of acid, and 1.5 million cubic feet of cylinder gases.

As the electronics industry expands and the technology used in semiconductor production advances, the use of hazardous chemicals is increasing. One estimate (by Strategic Analysis, a Reading, Pennsylvania, consulting firm) predicted in 1982 that the market for electronics chemicals would nearly double by 1987—from $2.24 billion to $4.05 billion per year. Advanced techniques for "doping" silicon wafers with arsine and phosphine use these poison gases in concentrations of 100 percent (unlike previous methods, in which the gases were greatly diluted). And with the race to develop ever faster microelectronic devices, a new kind of semiconductor made from gallium arsenide instead of silicon will increase the long-standing problem of exposure to carcinogenic arsenic.

With the use of so many toxic substances, the potential threats to worker health in the electronics industry are varied. The most visible and best understood are the one-time injuries or accidents such as acid burns. Hydrofluoric acid, used in etching wafers, can cross or penetrate the skin and cause severe damage to deep tissues. Dr. David Discher, a private occupational health consultant in Silicon Valley, has estimated that hydrofluoric acid burns bad enough to require surgery occur about once a month at each of the major semiconductor firms in the region.

Then there are the exposures to chemical fumes and gases produced by major spills or leaks. These can have acute respiratory effects, causing pulmonary irritation, "narcosis" or central nervous system depression, and, in the case of exposure to poisonous gases, even death. In a one-year period (from July 1979 to June 1980), the Palo Alto Fire Department reported fifty-nine leaks or spills requiring its assistance, more than one per week.

The most common hazards in the electronics industry are also the most difficult to detect—chronic low-level exposure to chemical solvents. Because such exposures accumulate slowly and because the symptoms they cause are often delayed or indirect, they are notoriously difficult to document or diagnose. Workers often don't know that they are being exposed. When they finally do become ill, they often don't realize that their illness is occupationally related.

And, in many cases, the precise relationship between chemical cause (or causes) and health effects is ambiguous and unclear.

"There are a wide array of symptoms, none of which is easily related to one specific exposure," explains Dr. Joseph LaDou, acting chief of the Division of Occupational and Environment Medicine at the University of California at San Francisco and probably the foremost medical authority on the hazards of the semiconductor industry. "In many cases, the symptoms are unknown," LaDou continues. "There are not the families or clusters of symptoms that make up recognizable 'syndromes' that doctors are familiar with in other areas of occupational medicine."

Sometimes, low-level solvent exposure causes skin irritation, rashes, or other dermatological symptoms. Often it can produce a variety of what LaDou calls "neuropsychological complaints" like headaches, dizziness, or memory loss (LaDou compares it to "low-grade inebriation"). But the most serious potential threat of these low-level exposures is the long-term effects. Many of the substances used in electronics are strongly suspected of causing cancer—for example, the solvent trichloroethylene or arsenic. Others are suspected reproductive hazards (the commonly used solvent xylene has been reported to cause menstrual irregularities, sterility, and toxemia in pregnant women). And the "synergistic" effects of exposure to a number of different workplace chemicals can go far beyond the effects produced by any single substance. The only way to determine precisely the degree to which high-tech workers are at risk would be to perform a comprehensive epidemiological study that tracked the occurrence of certain diseases in a sample population of high-tech workers against their occurrence in a control group. As yet, no major study of the health of high-tech workers exists.

Until it does, Joseph Ladou says that one can think of the toxic exposures in the electronics industry as forming a kind of pyramid. At the apex are the documented cases of work loss due to systemic poisoning. The actual numbers are small—according to the California statistics, approximately one hundred people per year in the semiconductor industry and about two hundred in electronics as a whole—but the percentages, compared to other industries, are extraordinarily high. Then there is a band of workers who have probably experienced systemic poisoning but who have not missed work, usually as a result of poor company health and safety practices, says LaDou. Finally, there is the vast majority of low-level exposures that cause no immediate symptoms—what LaDou calls "asymptomatic chronic chemical exposures." "We don't know how many of them there are," says LaDou. "But there is no production or maintenance worker in the industry who is not chronically exposed to chemicals."

One of the more controversial aspects of the occupational health hazards in Silicon Valley concerns the disease known as "chemical sensitization" experienced by Adele Perez. The term refers to a provocative theory put forward by a group of San Francisco Bay Area physicians who practice what they call "clinical ecology." After a major chemical exposure or a long series of low-level exposures, the theory holds, people can become "sensitized"—first to the chemical itself, then to a wide variety of other chemical substances that, in the course of the past fifty years, have become an integral part of modern life. This "sensitization" theory provides a single explanation for many of the symptoms experienced by electronics workers: unusually severe headaches (Adele Perez calls them "chemical headaches"); extreme fatigue ("you feel like gravity is three times what it really is," says one sufferer); a metallic taste in the mouth; rashes and blisters; even psychological symptoms such as irritability, depression, and memory loss. It has also been used to account for the observation that for some people these symptoms seem to continue long after the individual has left the workplace where the original exposure occurred.

"When you see these people just walking around, they look all right," says Mandy Hawes, a San Jose attorney who has represented some fifty current and former electronics workers in worker compensation and damage suits, concerning exposure to toxic substances in the industry. "One has the tendency to ask, 'What's wrong with him? He looks fine.' But these very same people who look okay might get headaches when they go to the gas station to fill up their car or, perhaps, around hair spray or perfume."

Dr. Allen Levin is a San Francisco immunologist who has examined and treated many electronics workers. He describes sensitization as a product of "immunological dysregulation." The immune system protects the human organism from threatening environmental agents (such as those found in viruses or bacteria) known as antigens. It operates by a complex process of chemical checks and balances between two classes of cells known as B cells and T cells. B cells produce the antibodies that attach themselves to antigens and neutralize their effect on the body. T cells serve as a governing mechanism that controls the production of antibodies by B cells.

For an idea of how the immune system normally operates, says Levin, imagine an automobile put into drive, its engine revving, but held stationary by the application of the brakes. In the immune system, "suppressor T cells" usually keep the antibody-producing B cells in check. However, when a person gets a virus, is exposed to bacteria, or comes into contact with something in the environment to which he is allergic, then the suppressor cells are temporarily weakened—the brakes on the automobile are released—and the proper antibodies are produced to attack the foreign agents entering the body's system.

When people become sensitized, Levin argues, the immune system goes haywire. "It's like a car where the brakes are slipping," he says. "People lose their capacity to discriminate" between an environmental agent that is dangerous and one that is not (a small quantity of some chemical, say, that in itself poses no real threat). As a result, the immunological system "starts making antibodies against damn near everything." And the individual acquires allergies—at first to the original chemical which triggered the disease, then to related substances. In some cases, says Levin, sensitization can even extend to the body's own hormones.

Levin claims that immunological dysregulation also helps explain the psychological symptoms that many victims of sensitization often display. Because of biochemical similarities between the immunological and neurological systems, he says, "psychological symptoms are very, very common in immunologically related diseases. When we look into psychosomatic and psychiatric disease, what we see is allergy. The behavioral aberrations are secondary to the immunological problem."

Once an individual becomes sensitized, says Levin, "the most important thing is to change your environment." To reverse the effects can take anywhere from eighteen months to two years—"just as long as you don't go back to the same heavily toxic environment." As for those who are "hypersensitized," adds Levin, "the disease never really goes away."

The sensitization thesis is extremely controversial in the Bay Area medical community. According to Joseph LaDou, clinical ecology is anything but "mainstream" medicine. "The clinical ecology cases aren't a significant fraction of the work-loss cases in electronics," says LaDou. "While there is some reason to believe they may be on the right track, they tend to go way beyond the existing scientific evidence." And Dr. Donald German, chief of the allergy department at the San Francisco Kaiser-Permanente Medical Center, criticizes the claims of the clinical ecologists as undocumented in the peer review literature or the product of poorly designed health studies. "As we have seen time after time, conclusions based on uncontrolled trials, single case studies, and anecdotal reports may impart a false impression of the effectiveness of the diagnostic procedure or a treatment, potentially misleading both the physician and the patient," says German. "There is no scientific basis for the veracity of their theories at this time."

But the debate over chemical sensitization is far more than a mere theoretical issue confined to the medical community. Part of the visibility of the immunological-dysregulation hypothesis is due to the use that plaintiff attorneys have made of it to prove disability in worker compensation suits brought by former electronics workers. "We're right on the edge of seeing a dollar explosion on this issue," says one Bay Area clinical ecologist who has served as an expert witness in some of these cases. "Basically, there is a Love Canal in a lot of those buildings. There is going to be an unbelievable explosion of litigation over the next few years."

In 1977, Marta Rojas was a forty-year-old chemist at Signetics, a Sunnyvale, California, semiconductor manufacturer. She performed topographical analysis of materials using an electron microscope. In the course of her job, Rojas worked with a variety of toxic chemicals—organic acids, xylene, arsenic gases, and trichloroethylene, just to name a few. In her five and a half years at the company, she had noticed the occasional severe headache but never imagined it might be work-related. Then, that September, Rojas experienced an exposure that would eventually drive her from Signetics and the electronics industry altogether. Her story would become one of the first cases to bring Silicon Valley's health and safety problem to public notice.

While Rojas was working in her laboratory, a gust of chemical fumes was blown back into her face by a defective exhaust hood. "It hit me just like a blow in the chest," she remembers. She developed blisters in her mouth and an acrid metallic taste. She had rashes on her skin, a painful sore throat, respiratory problems, and what seemed to be some loss of hearing. Over time, the most distressing symptoms were psychological. There were moments when Rojas felt she was losing control of her behavior. "It was a general feeling of being drugged," she explains. "I would feel 'possessed' somehow. I'd get very aggressive and then, after it passed, extremely tired."

Rojas was not the only person in the R&D facility who began suffering from these symptoms. At least two other workers—metallographers Cathy Bauerle and Kathi Hee—had them as well. Unlike the effects of a typical industrial accident, the symptoms persisted long after the original exposure. They would diminish when the women were away from the lab—on weekends, for example, or during vacations—only to worsen when they returned to work.

Over the next few months, Rojas, Bauerle, and Hee tried to convince Signetics management that there was an ongoing problem in the research and development lab. At first, they were met with skepticism. "They said, 'We've heard of this before,'" Bauerle remembers. "'We think it might be mass hysteria.'" At one point, a doctor in the local medical clinic attributed Rojas's persistent symptoms to a "viral illness." But the accumulation of evidence finally convinced Signetics management that there were indeed "fume problems" in the research facility. At that point, the company's skepticism was transformed into extreme caution.

The women were told not to tell any of their co-workers about their problems, for fear of causing alarm. They were also asked to help company safety personnel identify the location of toxic fumes. Because the women had become extremely sensitive to the presence of chemicals in the environment, they were used for a time as "human canaries" to help identify any large concentration of fumes. "They would take us to labs and say, 'Is there any problem in here?' " says Rojas. "We always tried to help because we wanted to have the problem fixed and go back to work." The procedure was discontinued, however, when Rojas nearly fainted after exposure to a particularly heavy dose of chemical fumes.

From late 1977 to the spring of 1978, the Signetics safety department ran a battery of tests to identify the source of the chemical exposures. Finally, in May 1978, the Environmental Research Corporation (a St. Paul, Minnesota, consulting firm called in to investigate) found that "the problem appears to be one of ventilation." Put simply, the ventilation system at the Signetics R&D facility inadvertently recirculated contaminated exhaust air back into the building. The exhaust systems for a number of wafer-fabrication areas vented onto the roof of the building—right next to the intake vent for the R&D lab which sucked "fresh" air in from the outside. To make matters worse, environmental regulations for the city of Sunnyvale required that unsightly exhaust vents be hidden from view. The decorative barrier installed around the edge of the roof had the unintended effect of creating a "toxic swimming pool." Under certain wind conditions, it trapped the exhaust fumes on the roof until they were pulled back down the intake vent to be dumped on Marta Rojas and the other workers in the lab.

Internal company memos give an idea of the kinds of exhaust being routed back into the research area as a result of this major flaw in building design. In May 1978, air samplings revealed significant concentrations of both trichloroethylene and xylene. In July, two wafer fabrication areas were out of compliance with local hydrocarbon pollution regulations. Another memo states that "TCE [trichloroethylene] is being used in unventilated conditions without proper personnel protective provisions." One manager described the continuing use of this carcinogenic solvent as "absolutely unconscionable" in the light of previous worker exposures.

For Rojas, Bauerle, and Hee, of course, the damage was already done. But their troubles at Signetics were not yet over. Unable to work in the contaminated research lab, they asked for positions in a chemical-free environment. Instead, they were shuttled from one location to another in the massive Signetics complex like so many silicon wafers in a tray. First, they were moved to a still largely vacant new building. But when some Xerox machines were moved in with them, chemicals in the ink provoked their allergic reactions. Then they were sent to an office-building conference room—until a high-level executive in a nearby office complained about the three women camped down the hall. Finally, in August 1978, they were "temporarily" moved to a Signetics cafeteria. There they would sit, eight hours a day, five days a week, for nearly a year, waiting for the jobs in the "nonchemical environment" that the company had intimated it would find for them but that would never materialize.

Marta Rojas remembers that year in the cafeteria as the worst part of her experience at Signetics. It was as if, having already been made to suffer once by their exposure, the women were being made to suffer again by being turned into scapegoats. They were given nothing to do; they just sat around tables all day. Rojas became convinced that the company was trying to make her and her colleagues quit. "They thought we were going to give up," she says. "They wanted us to quit; they as much as told us so." Managers would come into the cafeteria to tell them that if they didn't like it at Signetics, they were always free to find jobs somewhere else. Workers coming into the cafeteria for lunch would mutter about the three women goofing off. "It was as if they somehow resented our existence," says Rojas. "Some of them didn't believe us. Others knew we were right but didn't want to recognize it. They were too scared that it would happen to them."

Despite these pressures, the women refused to give up. And eventually they discovered that they weren't entirely alone. One day, a Signetics employee told them about a woman who had come down with similar symptoms, had taken a long leave of absence and was about to be laid off. When Rojas telephoned her, she learned that the woman had no idea that her health problems could be work-related.

"She always thought that she was the only one. None of the company nurses had told her that there were others with exactly the same problems."

Losing faith in Signetics's willingness to address their problem, the three women finally sought legal advice from San Jose lawyer Mandy Hawes in March 1979. The same month, they filed an official complaint with the National Institute of Occupational Safety and Health. Over the next six months, NIOSH industrial hygienists and doctors visited the Signetics site and gained limited access to employee health records. They eventually concluded (in a report released in February 1980) that there was a "significant occupationally related health problem" in the R&D lab. However, this partial vindication came too late for Marta Rojas, Cathy Bauerle, and Kathi Hee. In July, they were informed through their lawyer that they had been fired. The corporation decided that there was no safe place in any of its facilities where the women could work.

In the years since, the three women have pursued every possible path in order to receive compensation for their experience at the company. In September 1979, a California labor commissioner ruled that they had not been fired illegally as a result of a health and safety complaint. Ironically, while Signetics lawyers argued successfully before the commissioner that the real reason for the women's dismissal was that they were simply too sick to work, they subsequently contested the women's claims for worker compensation—even to the point of placing Marta Rojas under surveillance and surreptitiously filming her entrance into a photo copy shop and other "chemical" environments in an attempt to prove that she was not really sensitized to chemical substances.

The women also filed a complaint with the U.S. Department of Labor's Office of Contract Compliance, charging that the refusal of Signetics (a major defense contractor) to find them work in a non-chemical setting constituted discrimination against the physically handicapped and therefore violated federal regulations. The San Francisco bureau of the office found in the women's favor, but Washington chose not to pursue the investigation. Finally, the women joined with other former Signetics workers who had become ill while working at the company in a $25 million civil damages suit against the corporation, the manufacturer of the chemicals used in the plant, and the designer of the building in which the R&D facility was located. In 1982, Rojas, Bauerle, and Hee agreed to withdraw the suit against their former employer and to refrain from other action against the company in return for an undisclosed cash settlement—which, in the case of Marta Rojas, amounted to about one year's salary.

Despite the statistical evidence from doctors like Joseph LaDou and the experiences of workers such as Marta Rojas, Silicon Valley electronics companies have for the most part denied the existence of a serious occupational health problem in their industry. In fact, officials at the Semiconductor Industry Association, a San Jose–based trade group representing semiconductor manufacturers, have continued to boast that it is one of the safest in the nation. This viewpoint seemed to gain an official imprimatur in 1981. The first major study of health hazards in the semiconductor industry, conducted by California's Division of Occupational Safety and Health, found that the industry "consistently achieved notable records of occupational safety and health during the past decade," that there was "no evidence of chronic health hazards," and that those hazards which did exist "appear to be generally well-controlled."

But the impression that hazards are well under control in Silicon Valley is as false as the original notion that electronics is a clean industry. It is the product of the more or less systematic cooperation among industry, regulatory agencies, and portions of the medical community to downplay the seriousness of the health threat. It is a pattern of denial that keeps workers and the public in a state of ignorance and has so far prevented the Valley's toxic hazards from being adequately investigated.

One mechanism of denial is the system of occupational health care at the Valley's high-technology companies. With the exception of IBM (which has a research and semiconductor production facility in San Jose), none of the high-tech companies in Silicon Valley has a physician serving as full-time medical director on its staff. The usual practice is to hire industrial hygienists and in-plant nurses and then retain "consulting physicians" at one of the occupational health clinics in Santa Clara County. But this system has many serious flaws. For one, physicians who see electronics workers along with other patients rarely have the time or inclination to become expert in the complex health problems of the industry. For another, any physician who consistently finds occupational causes for workers' health problems runs the risk of losing his consultancy. Finally, most cases do not get to the consulting physician in the first place. They are treated in the workplace by company nurses, who are seldom trained in occupational health and whose primary responsibility, according to critics of occupational health care in the industry, is to keep problems inside the company.

Ironically, some of the recent studies of industry health hazards have become yet another mechanism of denial. In addition to the California study mentioned above, there have been two other reports on health hazards in the semiconductor industry, both funded by the National Institute of Occupational Safety and Health and carried out by private consulting companies. Based on industrial hygiene evaluations, company surveys, and occasional factory walk-throughs, they have generally reinforced the mild conclusions of the original California study.

But all these studies are entirely dependent on the industry they are examining—for information and even for access to company records and to the workplace itself. "They put someone into the industry who has to learn it from scratch," explains LaDou. "And by the time he knows what to look for, he has run out of time and money." As a result, he says, all the studies of the semiconductor industry done so far have been "dreadfully superficial."

The studies also suffer from the familiar problem of the revolving door between industry and the public agencies responsible for regulating them. "Whether they realize it or not," LaDou continues, "the regulators are really controlled by the industry they are looking at." The author of the 1981 California study that found "no evidence of chronic health hazards" is now director of health and safety at Advanced Micro Devices, a major semiconductor manufacturer. And the major impetus for the private consulting companies who do contract research for NIOSH is to develop the expertise that will lead to consulting contracts with the industry itself. The result, says LaDou, is "the clearest example of primrose-path science you could ever see." There is still no regional or national study on the actual health of high-technology workers. And with this "absolute vacuum of basic health research," says LaDou, it is easy for both industry and government to ignore the growing health problem. Until the electronics industry agrees to cooperate in a major health study of its workforce, "we're shadow-boxing around in the dark."

The pattern of denial even extends to the very basics of statistical record-keeping where one often finds the first hint that an industry has a health and safety problem. California collects some of the most thorough occupational health and safety statistics of any state in the nation. But the Semiconductor Industry Association has developed its own privately funded and controlled statistical data base. And when the numbers don't entirely correspond to the industry's image of itself, the association has not been above changing them—as a recent example suggests.

For statistical purposes, all industrial accidents are divided into two basic categories—"injuries" and "illnesses." Injuries have traditionally been defined as "instantaneous" events—a one-time accident or exposure such as a broken finger, an acid burn, or the splashing of chemicals into the eyes. Any workplace accident that is not instantaneous in this sense is considered an illness—for example, the prolonged exposure to a toxic chemical which results in respiratory problems.

At least, this *used* to be the accepted understanding of these terms until the Semiconductor Industry Association took it upon itself to change them. Upset by the high levels of occupational illness being reported for their industry, semiconductor executives decided in 1981 to broaden the meaning of "instantaneous" to include any workplace accident occurring "within a very short duration of time." According to this somewhat vague formulation, semiconductor firms began reporting as "injuries" such incidents as the inhalation of toxic gases, even when it was spread over several hours. Not surprisingly, the result was to lower substantially the occurrence of occupational illnesses as reflected in the California health statistics.

There was another advantage to this new reporting system. According to California law, "injuries" that do not result in lost work time do not have to be reported to Cal-OSHA, whereas *all* occupational illnesses do. Thus, if the industry could redefine certain exposures as injuries and, through the company nurse system, keep people on the job, then the number of incidents reported to state officials would be greatly reduced.

Industry representatives have justified this change with the argument that prior to 1981, many companies were actually overreporting industrial illnesses. To cite one example, they say that acid burns, which qualify as injuries even under the traditional definition, were often reported by companies as illnesses. Many health and safety professionals in the Silicon Valley region disagreed and asked the state to examine the practice. Investigators from Cal-OSHA reviewed the records of six major semiconductor firms in the Valley to discover that all of them were recording the inhalation of toxic fumes, even over quite long periods of time, as one-time injuries. Some of the firms were neglecting to record certain exposures altogether. In one case, a worker was exposed to toxic fumes for three to four hours, causing nausea and vomiting. By the time the company finally got around to sending him to a doctor, the symptoms had receded. The case was interpreted as simple first aid.

Both Cal-OSHA and the Semiconductor Industry Association turned to the federal government's Bureau of Labor Statistics for support in their dispute. In thirty-eight out of the forty examples presented to the bureau for interpretation, federal government statisticians sided with the state. However, California's Department of Industrial Relations eventually decided to drop its investigation of semiconductor industry reporting practices (under political pressure from the industry and the Reagan administration OSHA, critics have charged). As of this writing, California's semiconductor industry continues to record occupational illnesses and injuries according to the categories and the methods that it has defined.

But the high-tech industry's pattern of denial does its greatest damage in the workplace itself. All the practices described above encourage the very people most at risk—electronics production workers—to downplay the hazards they face. And, for those who do become sick from exposure to toxic chemicals used in industry, the experience is often a disturbing encounter with a special kind of powerlessness. It is not merely the vulnerability that losing control over one's health tends to engender, no matter what the cause. It is not even the fear accompanying the disquieting realization that the job one assumed to be safe is not. It is also what Joseph LaDou calls a "feeling of betrayal"—when the promise of the corporate community proves to be false.

Advanced Micro Devices (AMD) of Sunnyvale, California, is probably one of the most famous of Silicon Valley's enchanted corporations. The reputation of its founder and chief executive officer, Jerry Sanders, as a provocative and charismatic high-tech entrepreneur was unequivocally established in 1980 when he held a company-wide lottery—dubbed "the American Dream"—in which the winner, an AMD production worker, would receive $1,000 each month for the next twenty years. AMD has matched its high-tech image with solid financial success. With a compound growth rate of 30.8 percent between 1978 and 1983, it was the fastest-growing American producer of integrated circuits, the lifeblood of the computer revolution.

Recently, however, AMD's image has been tarnished by a bitter health and safety dispute. Several former company employees who worked in four of the corporation's semiconductor fabrication facilities in Sunnyvale are suing AMD for punitive damages; they charge the company with willful negligence in failing to protect them from toxic hazards they were exposed to on the job. Their stories suggest how Silicon Valley's health and safety crisis is experienced by workers on the shop floor.

Paula Baca is a classic example of the typical Silicon Valley female production worker. She began working in the semiconductor industry at the age of sixteen and has crisscrossed the Valley working at a host of companies (including National Semiconductor, Signetics, Synertek, Intersil, and, on three separate occasions, AMD). She has held the entire range of semiconductor fabrications jobs.

Before Baca came to work at AMD for the last time, in July

1980, she had experienced the usual accidents and exposures that have become relatively common in Silicon Valley. She had noticed occasional headaches and dizziness; she had even been hospitalized once, after hyperventilating during a chemical spill. Nevertheless, Baca never considered her work particularly dangerous. In this, too, she shared an attitude widespread among workers in the high-tech electronics industry.

"It was just something taken by everyone as being okay," Baca remembers. "It couldn't be dangerous if we're working with it— that's mainly what we thought. When you go into electronics, you think, They've been using this stuff for years, so it must be okay. It's not really talked about. Everybody acts like it's not a big deal."

When Baca started working on the night shift at AMD's Fab III production area, she encountered some of the worst working conditions in her entire career. There were frequent chemical spills, as often as two or three times every week. Ventilation was poor. There were laminar flow hoods to keep the air circulating in order to protect the sensitive silicon wafers from dust, but there were no exhaust hoods to vent toxic fumes away from the machines and out of the work area.

What previously had been only an occasional problem for Baca now became a source of nearly constant concern. She began to come down with horrendous headaches at the end of each workday. For the first time in her life, she started having menstrual problems. In general, she felt run down and exhausted, almost as if she never really felt well.

It got to the point where Baca found she could recognize the presence of certain chemical fumes in the workplace by the kind of symptoms they would provoke in her body. Xylene, for example, made her mouth go dry and her face itch. Time and again, she would go to her supervisor to say, "There's a xylene leak somewhere—I can taste it." But if no one could smell the fumes, nothing was done. Baca had to carry on despite her discomfort.

Then, on November 5, 1982, Baca had what she calls her "chemical accident." She was teaching a new worker how to operate a machine when, all of a sudden, she got an especially bad headache. "It got so bad it hurt just to move my eyes," she remembers. "Even the lights bothered me." Feeling dizzy, as if she were about to pass out, Baca complained once again to her supervisor. Neither he nor the area technician nor the lead operator could smell anything. Then, when another worker moved Baca's chair in order to change the tanks feeding chemicals into the machine, he discovered a puddle of xylene beneath it. Baca had been sitting on top of the spill for nearly four hours.

On her way home that morning, Paula Baca was so sick she had to pull over to the side of the freeway three separate times. Over the next few days, her symptoms seemed to subside somewhat when she was at home, only to return within half an hour or so once she came in to work. Baca went to a company nurse, who assured her that there was no serious problem, that she was well enough to work. But when Baca visited her own doctor, he put her on two weeks' disability and advised her never to work in an area where xylene was used again. Five days after returning to AMD after her disability period, Paula Baca was fired—ostensibly for a discrepancy on her time card relating to her visit to the company nurse. She believes she was dismissed because she took her health problems to a doctor outside the corporation. "They wanted to get rid of me because I went and saw a doctor," she says. "They didn't want me because of my illness. They probably figured I'd get another job and blame my future problems on someone else. But I won't."

Paula Baca believes that had she not been fired by AMD, she would still be working there today. When she first started in electronics, she was making around $4 an hour. By the time she came to AMD's Fab III, she was being paid more then $8—"real good money," she explains. "We were getting used to it." Even when workers do become aware of the hazards they face, their first tendency is a kind of denial—parallel to that of their employers. It is just too easy to keep on working or, perhaps, to move to another company in hopes that conditions there will be better. Besides, explains Baca, "everybody is worried about their job. They don't want to become known as a troublemaker. They don't want to get labeled."

Nancy Hawkes, who worked as a trainer in Fab III, did get labeled. Like Baca, she became sick after exposure to toxic chemicals.

She was eventually diagnosed as being chemically sensitized. But unlike most workers with health problems in the semiconductor industry, Hawkes tried to do something about it.

She began from a position of ignorance, an ignorance reinforced by the lack of information provided to workers about the substances they use in their work. "People don't know what they're working with because they're never *told* what they're working with," says Hawkes. "I was never informed of the hazards. Oh, I was told that I was working with acid and that it could burn me, yes. But I was never told about the possible carcinogens or the effects of solvent inhalation." At AMD, says Hawkes, chemicals were rarely labeled with their proper scientific name. Instead, they were put in bottles listing little information besides the part number and the process the chemical was to be used for. And she and other workers claim that the company's Chemical Handling Guide, which provided some information on the toxicity of chemicals and guidelines for their use, was not readily available for production workers.

So when Hawkes began to suffer from nausea and vomiting on the job, she, like others, did not connect her illness to her work. "All I knew was that I was sick," she remembers. "I thought maybe I was the only one." Hawkes was also three months pregnant at the time. When she went to the company nurse to complain about her symptoms, she was told that her sickness was probably due to her pregnancy.

As Hawkes's symptoms persisted (besides headaches and nausea, she was plagued by infections of her upper respiratory tract, bladder, ears, and eyes), she began to suspect another cause. And she started to learn what she could about the chemicals she was working with every day. Her first sources of information were the people she worked with. Others in the Fab area were suffering from similar complaints. She informally got hold of a copy of the Chemical Handling Guide from a maintenance supervisor. She even spent some time on the AMD loading dock where chemicals came into the plant from outside vendors. There she saw tanks of xylene ready to be moved into the factory. They had safety warnings complete with skull-and-crossbones stenciled on the side. But perhaps the most compelling revelation for Hawkes was when she talked about the chemicals she used with her brother-in-law, a biochemist. He couldn't believe some of the stories she told. "If he's getting so upset," Hawkes remembers thinking, "then there's got to be something wrong."

In her position as a trainer in Fab III, Hawkes tried to communicate some of her knowledge about toxic hazards to new AMD employees. She began to copy pages from the Chemical Handling Guide and hand them out with other training materials. She explained how solvents like xylene were potentially dangerous and that workers should be careful not to work around spills or where there were fumes in the air. As word about her advice to new employees got back to her supervisor, Hawkes's work evaluations began to drop. In her first three years at AMD, she had never had a rating below 95 out of 100. In six months, her performance ratings dropped to the low 20s. Ironically, her evaluation for "work knowledge" went from "excellent" to "unsatisfactory."

Then, one day, Hawkes ordered the evacuation of her trainees from the Fab III workplace after a major xylene spill. Despite the fact that she spent nine days on disability with lesions in her throat caused by inhalation of the xylene, she was accused of provoking "mass hysteria" and threatened with dismissal. In February 1981, Hawkes transferred out of Fab III to avoid continuing harassment from her supervisor. Ten months later, still suffering recurrent symptoms and having discovered that she was pregnant once again, Hawkes left AMD, fearing for her health and that of her child. Like Baca, she has been refused compensation by the corporation.

It would be difficult to label Anita Zimmerman as a "troublemaker." Before entering electronics, she had worked as a licensed vocational nurse for nine years in Kansas. So when she came to AMD in September 1980 it was only natural that she should decide to take the ten-week training course that qualified company employees for AMD's own Emergency Response Team. And yet, Zimmerman's experience also suggests how few resources workers have to protect themselves from the hazards of the high-tech workplace. Even those employees who were responsible for dealing with health and safety emergencies, she claims, did not have the power to protect workers on the job.

Zimmerman worked in Fab VI, at the time a research and development area where engineers tried out new production processes. On September 10, 1981, the area experienced the first in a series of chlorine gas leaks. As soon as she entered the workplace, Zimmerman remembers, she could tell that something was wrong. "The room smelled five times worse than a swimming pool," she recalls. However, even though Zimmerman was a member of the Emergency Response Team, she didn't have the authority to evacuate people from the area. Her supervisor was working on a different shift; the lead operator claimed she couldn't smell a thing. By the time a number of other supervisors were called over from nearby production areas and consensus was reached that indeed something was wrong, more than half an hour had passed. Workers were suffering from headaches, nausea, and stinging eyes. Zimmerman, one of the last people to leave the workplace, completely lost her voice.

During the next six weeks, the leaks continued, and Zimmerman became increasingly ill. Finally, in late October, she was hospitalized with acute bronchial asthma.

While AMD has refused to comment about the particulars of Baca's, Hawkes's, and Zimmerman's cases, the company has drawn attention to its current extensive safety program. Headed by the former employee of California's Division of Occupational Safety and Health who wrote the state's original report giving the semiconductor industry a clean bill of health, the AMD health and safety staff includes thirteen industrial hygienists who monitor workplace conditions and do worker training. However, the stories of these three former AMD workers reflect the kinds of problems that health and safety experts say are common in the semiconductor industry: the special role of company nurses in dismissing worker complaints; the lack of useful information available to workers about the chemicals they use; the ignorance on the part of most employees about the hazards they face and their own tendency to deny that toxic substances might be dangerous; and, when workers do try to actively protect themselves on the job, the tendency on the part of management to retaliate against "troublemakers," sometimes even firing them.

However, there are a few signs that because of the actions of workers like Paula Baca, Nancy Hawkes, and Anita Zimmerman, this situation is slowly beginning to change. Plaintiff attorneys are beginning to secure worker compensation benefits for workers in claims against electronics companies; in fact, a whole new legal field known as "toxic torts" has grown up around the health and safety issue. And, most recently, a new episode in the story of Silicon Valley's health hazards has taken place. It promises to break through the industry's pattern of denial once and for all.

The December 1984 methyl isocyanate leak at the Union Carbide pesticide plant in Bhopal, India, was a tragic reminder that toxic substances in the workplace at times represent a threat to public health as well. The communities of Silicon Valley have been living their own less dramatic but no less disturbing example of that fact. After chemicals are used in the semiconductor production process, they are stored as toxic wastes in underground storage tanks at companies throughout the region. Until the early 1980s, these wastes were as invisible as the tanks in which they were buried. That began to change in a brief four-month period in the winter of 1981–82 when nine separate cases of chemical leaks from eroding storage containers were discovered. Since then, the citizens of Silicon Valley have learned that chemical wastes are contaminating their groundwater and, in some cases, their public and private drinking-water wells.

The location of the leaks reads like some high-tech industry hall of fame: spills were discovered at Hewlett-Packard, AMD, Intel, IBM, Signetics, and Fairchild. The Signetics leak in February 1982 forced the temporary closing of three out of nine public wells in Sunnyvale. One of the Fairchild leaks (altogether, there were five, one at each of the company's five sites in the Valley) had concentrations of the suspected carcinogen trichloroethylene at 180,000 times the level necessary for triggering an official public health alert.

But the most dangerous contamination occurred at the leak discovered first, on December 4, 1981, at Fairchild's semiconductor production facility in South San Jose. During an undetermined period of time prior to its discovery, the leak had pumped at least 58,000 gallons of toxic solvents into the ground. The storage tank was only two thousand feet upstream from Well Thirteen of the Great Oaks

Water Company, the primary well of an interconnected water system serving some sixteen thousand households in a middle-class South San Jose neighborhood. The spill contaminated the aquifer feeding the well with various chemicals: levels of trichloroethane, another common industrial solvent that has been linked to cancer in laboratory animals, was at twenty-nine times the official safe standard. Later tests found concentrations of toxins in the water as much as eight hundred times the recommended levels.

But these leaks were only the beginning. Responding to an outcry of public concern, the San Francisco Bay Area Regional Water Quality Control Board began an Underground Tank Leak Detection Program in April 1982. Of the eighty sites that have been investigated so far, sixty-four indicate contamination of soil or groundwater or both. The board is further investigating fifty-seven of these sites where hazardous substances threaten to contaminate drinking water as well. In November 1984, the Environmental Protection Agency estimated that there are some thirteen hundred separate sources of groundwater contamination in Santa Clara County, two to three times more than agency officials had anticipated. While most of the chemical leaks originated at local gas stations, as many as three hundred occurred at high-technology manufacturing plants. The EPA has proposed making nineteen toxic sites in Santa Clara County eligible for the agency's "Superfund" priority list—more than any other county in the nation.

The clean-up of these and other leaks will certainly be enormously expensive. About two dozen electronics companies have already spent $80 million in clean-up and prevention costs, and EPA officials estimate the total costs to be four to five times higher. In South San Jose alone, it has cost Fairchild more than $16 million so far to develop eighty monitoring wells and twelve extraction wells simply to contain the spill (the corporation has also closed its South San Jose facility as well as three others in the Silicon Valley area). As of the summer of 1984, none of the leaks identified in the past three years has been entirely cleaned up.

The leaks have also revealed the inadequacy of previous efforts to regulate the electronics industry and to address the hazardous-waste issue. Despite the fact that between July 1979 and October

1980 California's Department of Health Services uncovered twenty-two on-site hazardous waste violations in Santa Clara County so serious as to require formal clean-up orders, the state agency was slow to develop procedures for evaluating company on-site storage plans. In November 1981, one month before the discovery of the first leak at Fairchild, California's auditor general's office issued a report highly critical of the department's efforts to identify and monitor hazardous waste sites.

Meanwhile, the electronics industry's refusal to admit that a serious problem exists and its aversion to any kind of public regulation has also been a major obstacle. At the same time that the state was urging stricter regulation of toxic substances at work, the Semiconductor Industry Association was trying to *soften* regulation. In October 1981, the association proposed changes in the Uniform Building Code that would have reduced the official classifications of many materials from "toxic" to the less stringent "inflammable." The proposed standards would also have allowed companies to store up to three times more chemicals in the workplace than current rules permit.

Normal practice of both industry and public officials was to keep information about chemical spills from the public. For example, when Fairchild discovered the massive leak in South San Jose, the corporation informed the water company (which closed down the well), but no one told the citizens who live in the affected neighborhoods. They had to wait for nearly two months before learning about the spill—from a newspaper article in the *San Jose Mercury*. Even the board of governors of the Regional Water Quality Control Board had to depend on the press to learn about many of the chemical leaks. The agency's staff had gotten into the habit of working directly with electronics companies on their storage problems; they neglected to inform either the public's representatives on the board or the public itself.

The publicity that the leaks have generated will make it extremely difficult to minimize Silicon Valley's toxic hazards ever again. Indeed, it has expanded public consciousness of yet another potential health threat—air pollution. The Bay Area Air Quality Monitoring Board has discovered not only that Silicon Valley firms are emitting tons of reactive organic gases into the atmosphere every day (the same fumes to which workers are exposed on the semiconductor production line), but that some of the industry's most prominent firms—including National Semiconductor, Intel, AMD, and once again Fairchild—had failed to acquire hundreds of necessary construction permits from the board or even to register with the agency in the first place. Some buildings and entire plants were built without the approval or review of the appropriate public agencies. The board has since established stringent pollution-control requirements for the semiconductor industry (the first in the nation) which mandate the reduction of solvent emissions by 90 percent by 1988.

In February 1984, the EPA began a two-year $950,000 program to study the entire range of environmental health hazards in the Silicon Valley region. And EPA policymakers have asked the National Institute of Occupational Safety and Health to further investigate potential health dangers for workers in the electronics industry.

Cleaning up Silicon Valley's toxic hazards will be expensive, but perhaps the biggest cost for the area's high-technology firms has been the shattering of their carefully crafted image as an alternative to the traditional industrial workplace. What one Fairchild executive called "a public relations nightmare" has led many citizens in the Valley to reevaluate their assumptions about the industry as an employer and a corporate neighbor. For many, this reevaluation has been accompanied by surprise, even shock. "I remember being so happy that we were having clean industry come into the community," San Jose's then mayor, Janet Gray Hayes, told the *San Jose Mercury* at the time when the first chemical leaks were coming to light. "I remember thinking about the smokestacks at other industries around the country. I didn't expect this problem to erupt in my own community." Other residents were not caught so naively off guard—in particular, those who had some experience with or knowledge of the electronics industry's toxic materials as an occupational hazard. The Silicon Valley Toxics Coalition, an association of labor and environmental groups, was instrumental in making sure that the "model ordinance" formulated to regulate waste storage in Santa Clara County contained provisions for the public disclosure of information and the protection of "whistle-blowers" at local firms. (In the original version of the bill, it was a felony for employees to reveal any of the chemicals being used by firms in the county.) In South San Jose, citizen activism has taken another form. Alarmed at the evidence of a cluster of birth defects in the area which they believe are related to the contamination of local drinking water, some five hundred neighborhood residents (nearly half of them children suffering from congenital heart defects, skin disorders, and other medical problems) have filed a multimillion-dollar lawsuit against Fairchild, the Great Oaks Water Company, and various other co-defendants, charging them with negligence in connection with the South San Jose spill. In January 1985, the California Department of Health Services released an epidemiological study that, without specifically linking the results to the Fairchild leak, reported levels of miscarriages and birth defects in the contaminated neighborhood at two to three times the rates observed in a carefully selected "control" area.

What explains the overwhelming failure of Silicon Valley's high-technology corporations to prepare adequately for the health hazards of their industry, and to protect their employees and the surrounding communities from them?

The relative youth of the microelectronics industry and the spectacular rapidity of its rise almost certainly helped to push concerns about health and safety into the background. In the heady rush toward the future, what could be easier than to neglect proper permits, hastily occupy poorly designed buildings, reflexively oppose public regulation of corporate practices? Even today, the semiconductor industry still invests less than 1 percent of its revenues in occupational health and safety activities. (By contrast, firms in "mature" industries generally spend 2.5 to 3 percent.)

The intense competition among Valley firms and their stringent secrecy about exotic and rapidly changing production processes probably also contribute to the failure. When a firm's competitive edge may depend upon "trade secrets" about the substances used in production, why inform and educate workers about the chemicals they use on the shop floor? And when the average selling price of an integrated circuit has fallen about 30 percent every year for the past twenty years—creating enormous pressures for cheap, efficient, and fast production—better to churn out wafers than to stop the production line every time someone detects a leak or spill.

The high mobility and ease with which workers move from one company to another in the industry is surely another crucial factor. When the chances are good that people with health complaints will simply move on to another workplace or leave the industry altogether, it is easy to ignore worker complaints, to marginalize the "troublemakers," and, in some cases, to exclude them entirely by forced dismissal.

But one other compelling consideration helps explain this failure of corporate responsibility. Silicon Valley's most prominent corporate leaders seem to believe so profoundly in their own ideology that they have persuaded themselves their industry truly *is* a place apart, protected from the usual risks of the work world by the special grace of high technology and the enchanted corporation. If so, then the very notion that the workplaces of Silicon Valley could be dangerous to the people who work in them would be, quite simply, unimaginable, contradicting their deeply held vision of what their world is like.

Whatever the reason, each leads to the identical conclusion. In order to avoid such failures in the future, our lives in the brave new workplace must become a public issue, which is to say, a political issue. Put simply, can we imagine a workplace where the private corporation does not hold a monopoly of power over work and technology and the uses to which it is put? Where workers, communities, the public at large all have a say, independent of the corporation itself? Confronted with the most comprehensive transformation of working life in more than fifty years, can we fashion a workplace where the conflicts of interests that will inevitably arise between workers and their employers, between private corporation and public commonwealth, can be expressed, negotiated, and ultimately resolved?

To do so means first to recognize that work is fundamentally a relationship of power and of conflict—an idea with a long history, and yet one that the current celebration of the enchanted corporation has tended to eclipse. Nevertheless, it is an idea that one continues to hear expressed, especially by workers on the front line of the brave new workplace.

"It was because we spoke up that they made it hard on us," says Anita Zimmerman, the nurse turned production worker at AMD. "They allowed us to learn a little more than the average worker, but we didn't forget where we came from. We didn't forget that we were still operators and weren't the same as management. We informed people about their rights and their privileges, about what they should know and should be able to make choices about. That's why they made it so hard on us. Because we had decided that, when it came to our health and safety, we weren't company."

"They want to present an image, but it's phony," says Marta Rojas, who has moved from Sunnyvale in the flatlands of the Santa Clara Valley to a house in Belmont, at the very peak of the mountain ridge that runs north of Palo Alto toward San Francisco. She is still sensitized, and the frequent ocean breezes make the air fresher up there. "Working in the industry, you feel part of the computer revolution," Rojas continues. "I used to think, Boy, they do such fantastic things with computers. And, of course, some of the applications of the technology really are fantastic. But when I start thinking of all these low-quality mass-production chips—what they call 'jelly beans,' the kind that go into Atari video games—that's when I get furious. To think that people are getting sick just so some kid can play his stupid Atari game!"

In their own way and in their own words, Zimmerman and Rojas identify the conflict that has shaped their working lives. Whether the issue is health and safety, new technology, the organization of work, or the very purpose of the corporation itself, the problems of the brave new workplace can be resolved only when the conflicts of interest that swirl around these issues and give them their texture and their weight are brought into the open, made matters of public discussion, debate, even controversy. To do so requires creating new modes of political discourse and new kinds of social institutions. Indeed, it requires nothing less than a new system of industrial relations in American society as a whole.

PART THREE

THE
SOCIAL CONTROL
OF
TECHNOLOGY

CHAPTER SEVEN

LABOR'S MUTED VOICE

ONE OF THE MOST SUCCESSFUL WAYS for people to defend themselves against the abuses of corporate power at work has been to form their own independent institutions in the workplace. The history of American trade unionism is the story of how workers have struggled to achieve collectively what is so very difficult to obtain individually: a measure of real power and control over working life. In a recent book entitled *What Do Unions Do?* two Harvard economists, Richard Freeman and James Medoff, capture the quality of this fundamental motivation of unionism. What unions do, they argue, is to provide workers with a "collective voice."

In the absence of such a voice, people have remarkably few options for resolving conflicts of interest at work. Of course, one can always try to make one's own grievances known, to fight individually for better wages, working conditions, and the like. But such isolated challenges to corporate power are too ineffective, the possibility of retaliation too great, to make this an option that people resort to frequently. As former electronics worker Paula Baca says, "people are afraid for their jobs."

Far more common is to express one's dissatisfaction by leaving—what the sociologists call "exit" (and Peters and Waterman term simply "opting out"). This is the classic method for expressing preferences in a market economy. It requires that one treat work like a commodity, the same way one responds to a bad restaurant or a shoddy pair of shoes. One takes one's business elsewhere. Of course, the effectiveness of this approach to workplace conflicts depends entirely on one's position in the labor market. What may be feasible for the individual whose skills are in great demand (the Silicon Valley computer engineer, say) is little more than an abstract chimera for a great many workers in America today.

"Voice" is the antithesis of "exit." It implies an altogether different conception of work—not as a commodity but as a social activity. The presence of a union opens up far more choices for workers. They no longer have to "buy into" or "opt out of" an undesirable work situation; they can actually try to change it, to make it better. Through voice, write Freeman and Medoff, people can try "to bring actual and desired conditions closer together." They can also gain access to a variety of "public goods"—like health and safety—which competitive markets consistently undervalue and ignore. In this way, workers become less dependent on their individual position in the labor market. They introduce new social criteria—their own—into the decisions shaping working life.

"The collective nature of trade unionism," Freeman and Medoff write, "fundamentally alters the operation of the labor market and, hence, the nature of the labor contract. . . . As a result, management power within enterprises is curtailed by unionism, so that workers' rights are likely to be better enforced. . . . As a collective voice unions . . . fundamentally alter the social relations of the workplace."

What's more, unionism has an economic function. When workers gain a measure of influence over management decision-making, this tends to improve the overall efficiency of the work organization. Collective bargaining, formal grievance procedures, the informal contacts between union officials and managers all constitute a wealth of information about worker attitudes, interests, and skills. When management pays attention to this information and uses it "to learn about and improve the operation of the workplace and the production process, unionism can be a significant plus to enterprise efficiency." Based on their analysis of quantitative data on the American economy, Freeman and Medoff conclude that "the view of unions as a major deterrent to productivity is erroneous. In many sectors, unionized establishments are more productive than nonunion establishments."

Finally, unionism's collective voice also transcends the individual workplace, the particular corporation, and even the specific union to which an individual belongs. By linking workers to a society-wide labor "movement," it gives them a say in society as a whole and a means to shape it according to a broader social vision. This idea of unionism as a social movement—best captured in the venerable labor term "solidarity"—even reaches beyond labor's own members to embrace wide sectors of society not organized into unions, in particular its most marginal groups. At times, labor's social movement even translates workers' collective power in the workplace into political power in society as a whole.

And this too changes how we think about and understand work. It's not merely a private activity to be shaped by managers representing the interest of the private corporation. It's a public activity which contributes to the wider society and, as such, ought to be responsive to broader social concerns. Thus, when it comes to considering how best to address the problems of the brave new workplace, a logical place to begin is with what has been the most effective vehicle for "collective voice" in the workplace in the past: the institutions of American trade unionism.

And yet even the most casual observer of the American labor movement has to recognize that unionism in America faces a profound crisis—what Freeman and Medoff term the "slow strangulation of private-sector unionism." In the mid-1950s, unions represented some 34 percent of the private-sector nonagricultural labor force. By 1980, the proportion had dropped to 24 percent, a decline "unprecedented in American history." In the depths of the 1982 recession, union membership plunged even lower, to below 20 percent, for the first time since the depths of the Great Depression.

The figures from union organizing elections, held under the auspices of the National Labor Relations Board, are even more dramatic. In the 1950s, unions were successful in about three-quarters of the organizing elections administered by the NLRB. Approximately 1 percent of the total U.S. labor force was unionized this way every year. By the early 1980s, however, unions were engaged in so little organizing and winning so few NLRB elections that a meager .14 percent of the total workforce was being organized each year.

To make matters even worse, in recent years the American business community has mounted a concerted attack on unionism's economic gains, political power, and social legitimacy. At the collective-bargaining table, more and more companies have demanded wage and work rule concessions, announced plant closings and "bankruptcies" to get out of union contracts, and pushed for new measures to break down union solidarity such as dual wage systems (in which new employees are paid at lower wage rates than plant veterans). In government, American corporations joined together to defeat union-sponsored revisions of U.S. labor law in 1978; and the Reagan administration has let some of the most important federal protections of union activity (particularly in the area of union organizing and occupational safety and health) go unenforced.

But the most pernicious sign of labor's declining legitimacy in the eyes of American corporations has been the growing willingness of companies to go to the length of violating federal law in order to combat union organizing drives. From 1960 to 1980, the number of NLRB elections every year remained relatively constant, but charges of unfair labor practices filed against employers rose fourfold (those that involved the dismissal of workers for union activity tripled). Freeman and Medoff estimate that in 1980, one out of every twenty workers who favored the union in NLRB elections was fired for union activity. There is roughly one case of discharge ruled illegal by the NLRB for every labor board representation election.

Finally, labor's role appears to be most marginal in the brave new workplace that has been the subject of these pages. Despite Silicon Valley's health and safety hazards, few workers there or in other centers of high-tech industry see unionism as a practical alternative to the problems they face. The vast majority of firms in America's most technologically intensive industries are nonunion. In already unionized industries, the technological changes and management practices described in previous chapters are challenging the very foundations of union power—cutting into membership levels, eroding union bargaining units and occupational categories, and undermining traditional skills, work rules, and union tactics such as the strike. With these changes has come an increasingly widespread perception that unions have, somehow, become outmoded and obsolete—at best, irrelevant to the concerns of a new generation of workers and the issues of a new kind of workplace; at worst, a serious obstacle to technological change and economic competitiveness.

Should these current trends continue, by the end of the present decade American unionism may face what Freeman and Medoff call a "disastrous decline." If so, the implications will be far-reaching, not only for organized labor, but for American society as a whole. At the very moment when we are entering a period of massive technological and economic change, with enormous potential for disruption, conflict, and social costs, both inside the workplace and out, workers may be bereft of the one institution that has successfully represented their collective interests in the past. At a time when the American economy is facing its greatest challenge perhaps since the Great Depression, the absence of a strong union movement in the brave new workplace could ultimately have serious economic costs as well. But most disturbing of all is the possibility that we shall lose the distinctive social vision that has been organized labor's greatest contribution to American society—the conviction that work is a supremely public activity and that the workplace, like any other institution in our society, should be open to democratic decision-making and choice.

The current crisis of the American labor movement is intimately connected to the economic and technological transformations described in these pages. To understand how, one must first go back to the Great Depression, when the present form of American unionism took shape and the distinctive system of American industrial relations was created. That system has remained relatively unchanged up to the present day. But now the realities of the brave new workplace have shaken its foundations and challenged its *raison d'être* for the first time in half a century.

In the period between the First World War and the Depression, American unionism faced a challenge to its very survival not all that dissimilar from the one it confronts today. The changes in the economy and in the technology of production which had started in the late nineteenth century and reached their culmination during World War I undermined the traditional organization of unions along craft lines. The final triumph of scientific management during and immediately after the war eroded the principle of craft control in a variety of industries. And the rapid growth of new mass-production industries created whole new categories of workers—the semiskilled operatives of the assembly line—who did not fit easily into traditional craft occupations.

Throughout the 1920s, organized labor faced what Freeman and Medoff call a "two-pronged attack by management." On the one hand, some of America's largest and fastest-growing corporations were combining the production techniques of scientific management with paternalist labor relations and in-house "company unions" in a system known as "welfare capitalism." The idea that the corporation could meet the needs of the new workers of mass production industry in ways that the craft unions never could became widespread. On the other hand, the "American shop" movement began promoting an aggressive antiunionism throughout the business community—even to the point of using violence and coercion against union organizers and sympathizers.

As a result, union membership plummeted from the heights it had reached during the war. And by the early 1930s, there was a generalized perception that organized labor had no place in the dynamic new mass-production economy. "American trade unionism is slowly being limited in influence by changes which destroy the basis on which it is erected," George Barnett, president of the American Economic Association, told that body's annual meeting in December 1932. "I see no reason to believe that American trade unionism will ... become in the next decade a more potent social force."

Of course, just a few years later, that is precisely what happened. Amid the economic and social turmoil of the Great Depression, American workers created a broad-based social movement and inaugurated perhaps the most militant period of industrial conflict and labor organizing in the twentieth century. They established large and powerful unions in each of the heretofore "unorganizable" mass-production industries, such as auto, rubber, and steel. They articulated a new conception of solidarity based not on craft traditions and skills but on the common interests of all workers in a particular industry, no matter what their specific job category. And they created new kinds of institutions and practices ideally suited to the mass-production environment of giant factories and bureaucratic corporations—in particular, the plant-wide local union and the sit-down strike. In the process, they invented a new social vision and a new kind of union organization, what we have come to know as "industrial unionism."

Industrial unionism was, first and foremost, a response to the abuses of scientific management and the system of bureaucratic control that had been developing over the previous fifty years. The chief catalyst of the 1930s strikes, historian Mike Davis has written, was "the petty despotism of the workplace incarnated in the capricious power of the foreman and the inhuman pressure of mechanized production lines." In response, the new industrial unions developed a series of practices and protective measures designed to restrain arbitrary management authority by explicitly defining the rights and duties of workers at every step of the production process. This emphasis on negotiating with management the particular characteristics of each individual job became known as "job control" unionism.

The typical union contract became an elaborate description of each specific job in the mass-production factory. It spelled out wage rates and work rules, the proper procedures for layoffs and promotions (based primarily on seniority), even the speed of the assembly line itself. At the same time, industrial unionism also established an institutional framework of "industrial jurisprudence" to police this union contract, enforce agreements between labor and management, and adjudicate grievances and complaints. The major mechanism for this, on the union's side, was the shop steward system of the union local and the formal grievance procedure.

By "rationalizing" the Taylorist system, industrial unionism provided workers with a measure of control over work. And yet, in many respects, it was itself an offspring of the age of scientific management. The very idea of union "job control" was based upon the extreme specialization of labor and fragmentation of work inherent to Taylorism. In fact, unions came to depend upon the same Taylorist techniques of measurement, such as time and motion studies, to support their own claims for particular wage rates and work rules.

Industrial unionism also came to accept the classic Taylorist division between the execution of work and its design and the separation of the workforce between those who planned the production system and those who occupied the slots within it. This principle was enshrined in the idea of "management prerogatives" that became a standard part of most union contracts after the Second World War. In exchange for the right to become the exclusive bargaining agent for workers, industrial unions ceded to management the sole right and responsibility to direct production, introduce new technology and work processes, and, in general, determine the overall organization of work.

This had the effect of placing a wide range of corporate decisions—about technology and job design, investment and plant location, and other issues—largely outside the sphere of collective bargaining. To the degree that unions were able to influence such decisions, they did so indirectly and "after the fact"—always in response to management-initiated plans. This peculiar double quality—in one sense, challenging the corporate control of work; in another, sharing in its most fundamental premises—became the defining characteristic of industrial unionism. As we shall see, it has come back to haunt organized labor in the brave new workplace today.

But industrial unionism also had an economic function that proved crucial to the future development of the American economy. The MIT economist Michael Piore has argued that the economic crisis of the Great Depression was due, in part, to a fundamental contradiction between the requirements of mass production and the institutional arrangements of the American economy in the early twentieth century. The new mass-production industries were the most powerful and most productive form of industrial organization ever created, but they were dependent on one basic condition—the existence of stable markets and mass consumption in order to absorb the vast quantity of products they manufactured. Normally, large corporations tried to assure this stability by orchestrating demand (for example, through advertising) and administering prices. In periods of economic crisis, however, they were forced to fall back on what, at the time, was the primary mechanism for ensuring profitability and competitiveness in a laissez-faire capitalist economy: to lower prices by cutting employee wages. But this, of course, undermined the very capacity for mass consumption on which the economic system as a whole depended.

The Depression was one vast downward spiral in which progressive wage cuts and corresponding economic stagnation fed upon each other. As individual firms resolutely pursued their own immediate interests by cutting the wages of their workers, they all contributed to the breakdown of the system as a whole. And America's fabulously productive mass-production system almost came screeching to a halt.

Industrial unionism provided a way out of this impasse. It became the cornerstone of a new institutional system in the American economy that ensured the long-term stability of mass production. By negotiating and enforcing national contracts covering all the unionized workers in a particular industry, industrial unionism effectively took wages out of competition. Under the "pattern bargaining" of the U.S. auto industry, for example, workers at Chrysler received a wage package equivalent to that of their colleagues at General Motors or Ford. And the settlement in the auto industry also set the pattern for those in other unionized mass-production sectors. Under the national agreement between the United Mineworkers union and the Bituminous Coal Operators Association, the historical wage differential between miners in the north and miners in the south was finally erased. The solidarity of industrial unionism meant that workers could no longer be set against each other in order to serve narrow and shortsighted corporate interests. At the same time, the effect of mass unionization, writes Piore, was to "place a floor under the wage rate in an economic downturn and ... insure, generally through wage-setting procedures, that national consumer purchasing power expanded at a rate required to absorb the growing output generated by the further division of labor."

Thus, by the 1950s, industrial unionism had become a crucial part of a new system of industrial relations—accepted by corporate management (however grudgingly) as a guarantor of economic stability and legitimized and institutionalized by U.S. labor law. This institutional framework laid the foundation for the relatively stable expansion of the American economy in the post–World War II era and became a bulwark of newfound prosperity for whole sectors of the American population. For the next quarter-century, the militant social movement of the 1930s would be a key component in the development of the American corporate capitalist system.

Piore's description of unionism's role in stabilizing mass production also provides an intriguing explanation for the crisis of American labor today. The system of industrial relations founded on scientific management and mass production, on the one hand, and industrial unionism and detailed union "job control," on the other, worked fine as long as the U.S. economy remained dominant at home and abroad and the technology of mass production remained relatively unchanged. However, the economic and technological changes of the past decade have caused this institutional framework to unravel.

The mass-production system has expanded beyond the boundaries of any single country. As its techniques spread, the low-wage countries of the Third World have a fundamental competitive advantage. International competition has not only undermined the capacity of unions in this country to maintain and protect their own wages, it has introduced extreme competition, instability, and economic stagnation similar to that which occurred during the Great Depression, only this time on a global scale. At the same time, the development of new technologies based upon the computer have made possible entirely new kinds of work organization founded upon the principle of "flexible specialization." But for such systems to work effectively, management has to give up many of the traditional assumptions about economic efficiency associated with scientific management.

These changes have enormous implications for industrial unionism. As corporations try to adapt to this new economic environment, more and more managers have come to see unionism not as a force for stability but as an obstacle to industrial restructuring. "To a very large extent, the practice of American industrial unionism has come to rest upon, indeed to presuppose, Taylorism," Piore writes. "If technological efficiency is no longer carried by, or consonant with, Taylorism, it is easy to understand why a labor movement which presupposed that form of management should become increasingly irksome to employers."

So much so that today American unionism faces yet another "two-pronged attack by management." Only this time it is the enchanted corporation that promises to provide for workers' needs in the brave new workplace by replacing the bureaucratic rules and regulations of the union contract with the good feelings, high commitment, and trust of the corporate culture. And on the other hand, corporations in the traditionally unionized sectors of the economy have embraced a kind of "technological antiunionism" in which new technology is used systematically to erode union power and the work rules and collective-bargaining agreements created over half a century of negotiation and bargaining—all in the name of increased "flexibility."

Almost from the inception of industrial unionism, technology has been the Achilles' heel of union control in the workplace. Contrary to popular assumptions, American unions have rarely opposed technological change in the post–World War II era. According to the logic of "management prerogatives," they have accepted the corporation's right to introduce new technology and new production processes as it saw fit. Then, through collective bargaining, they have attempted to gain their fair share of the positive benefits of technology, primarily through productivity-related wage gains, and to protect their members from technology's costs, by means of a variety of contract provisions forbidding technology-related layoffs and downgrading or providing supplemental unemployment benefits, transition allowances, early retirement plans, and the like.

Such measures can cushion the negative impacts of technological change. When the scope of that change is relatively limited or short in duration, they can prove to be extremely effective. However, there is an important difference between "protecting" workers from the consequences of management decisions about technology and providing them with actual influence or control over the decisions themselves. Unions have rarely played a major role in the actual design or planning of technological change. Their approach to new workplace technology, as to other areas of management decision-making, has been reactive and after-the-fact. Because unions have been consistently on the defensive in this crucial area, their ability to exercise initiative on technology-related issues (let alone to provide alternatives to management plans) has been limited. And when the impacts of new technology have spread to entire work organizations or industries, they have created problems beyond the capacity of discrete protective measures to address. In such situations, the inability of unions to confront the technology issue directly has meant an overall erosion of union control.

Consider the example of what was perhaps the most militant and resourceful of the unions in the industrial union movement—the United Mine Workers. During the 1930s, UMW leader John L. Lewis had played a central role in the founding of the CIO; during the Second World War, he had pursued a course of labor militancy which brought the union into conflict not only with the coal industry but with the U.S. government. The UMW's militancy paid off; in the years after the war, the miners' contract had some of the most progressive provisions of any union contract in America. And yet in the 1950s, Lewis agreed to the widespread mechanization of coal mining that would eventually put massive numbers of miners (union and nonunion alike) out of work.

The logic of Lewis's decision to accept the mechanization of the mines fit squarely into the framework of industrial unionism at the time. The rise of cheap oil as an alternative source of energy after the war was placing severe competitive pressure on the coal industry. By forcing poorly capitalized companies (who could not afford the necessary investments for the new technology) out of business and dramatically improving productivity at the rest, mechanization would both improve the industry's competitiveness and make possible higher wages for union members. And yet, higher wages for some union workers were purchased at the price of unemployment for others. Because of the rationalization of the coal industry achieved through mechanization, two-thirds of the miners working in the coal industry in 1948 were displaced by 1969—with implications that went far beyond the UMW to affect the regional economy of the entire Appalachian region.

Mechanization also had negative impacts for those miners who continued to work. The vast numbers of unemployed miners desperate for work tended to undermine the ability of the union to enforce work rules in the face of management opposition. Moreover, the new technologies of "continuous mining," because they produced far more coal dust than previous work methods, actually contributed to an increase in occupational diseases such as pneumoniconiosis, or black lung. Whatever the gains enjoyed by some miners, they were offset by the overall erosion of union control and the creation of new kinds of problems.

Another example is the "mechanization and modernization" (M&M) agreements negotiated in the West Coast longshoring industry in the 1960s. In effect, the members of the International Longshoremen's and Warehousemen's Union (ILWU) gave up their considerable control over working conditions of their industry in exchange for a $25 million fund providing for early retirement, no layoffs, and a guaranteed minimum work week. The M&M agreements were a significant improvement on the deal that Lewis had struck in the coal industry; at the time, they were lauded as a socially responsible way to handle automation. However, the plans also divided the unionized workforce into two categories; senior workers were protected at the expense of younger workers in the industry. Once again, technological change came at the price of union solidarity. And the union ceded to management's plan for technology without any real effort to influence the direction that technological change took.

This same pattern has continued up to the present. Faced with company plans to eliminate more than 100,000 jobs in the next decade through new technology and foreign "outsourcing," the United Auto Workers in 1984 negotiated a pioneering job security provision with General Motors. The cornerstone of the plan was a $1 billion "job bank" to operate over the next six years. Workers with more than one year seniority who are displaced by new technology or outsourcing will be eligible to participate in the program; the job bank will pay their normal wages while they receive retraining or wait to be placed in new jobs in the corporation.

The plan is an improvement on previous job security provisions, but it was a considerable retreat from union demands made in negotiations for a role in company decision-making about new technology and the shift of production abroad. The final contract leaves the corporation free to pursue these strategies without any consultation with the union. Over the six-year life of the job-bank program, even $1 billion amounts to only $167 million each year—about the cost of one new paint shop in the U.S. auto industry. If attrition levels at GM continue at normal rates and some 45,000–50,000 workers resign or retire during the six-year period, then the job bank should be able to preserve the jobs of other workers displaced by technology. But the provision does not protect those laid off because of reductions in sales volume or decision to buy or produce cars abroad, which could cost the Autoworkers union tens of thousands of jobs.

Thus, despite improvements in union efforts to protect their members from the impacts of technological change, the fundamental issue of managerial control over new workplace technology has remained largely unchallenged. As the computerization of work extends into more and more workplaces, however, some unionists are beginning to question the adequacy of this traditional approach. They talk about fashioning a less reactive and defensive technology policy, one that allows them to take the initiative on technological issues in ways they have rarely done in the past.

So far, this aspiration has developed in a contradictory way. Taking the initiative on technology requires challenging the idea of "management prerogatives" and defining technological change not merely as a matter of "impacts" to be protected against but as a fundamental issue of union power and control. But the most comprehensive union attempts to do so have tried to achieve these goals through the same framework of "participation" and "labor-management cooperation" described in previous chapters. When the union desire for real influence over workplace technology meets the narrow forms of participation common at most corporations, the result is a collision of perspectives and interests. It may represent the distinctive form of labor conflict in the brave new workplace for years to come.

The workers of the American telecommunications industry have experienced the full range of problems associated with the brave new workplace, and because, unlike other high-tech sectors, their industry is substantially unionized, they offer an illustrative example of the difficulties facing unions struggling with the technology issue.

The Communications Workers of America (CWA) is the largest of the three major telecommunications unions.* In the past few years, it has acquired a reputation as one of the most forward-looking of American unions on technology and other issues of the changing workplace. In 1979, the CWA held the first national union conference on technology as a new labor issue. In 1982, the union even created a special Committee of the Future to explore the role of unionism in the Information Age.

Like other American unions, those of the telecommunications industry have negotiated a variety of defensive mechanisms over the years to protect their members from the negative impacts of techno-logical change. For example, the CWA's contract with the operating companies of the former Bell System includes a Reassignment Pay Protection Plan, protecting workers with seniority of fifteen years or more from downgrading due to technological change, and a Supple-mental Income Protection Plan, providing special payments to work-ers who accept early retirement as a result of the introduction of new technology. However, by the late 1970s, the increasing computeriza-tion of work in telecommunications and growing problems of job pressures and occupational stress had led to considerable rank-and-file discontent. Union leaders began to search for a new approach to such issues, what one CWA report calls a "reshaping and rethink-ing" of union technology policy.

At the same time, managers at AT&T were expressing their own concerns. The stress epidemic of the late 1970s had sent employee morale plunging, as the responses to AT&T's Work Relationships Survey indicated. As corporate managers looked toward the increas-ing deregulation of the telecommunications industry and the possi-ble divestiture of AT&T, they began to worry that company employees were ill prepared for the demands of rapid change and the new, highly competitive markets that management hoped to enter.

These two sets of concerns came together in the 1980 Bell Sys-tem collective-bargaining negotiations. AT&T and the three unions

---

* The others are the Telecommunications International Union (TIU) and the International Brotherhood of Electrical Workers (IBEW). The following pages draw on the experience of the CWA and TIU.

of the industry established a network of joint labor-management committees designed to address some of the problems associated with the rapidly changing telecommunications workplace. A National Committee on Joint Working Conditions and Service Quality Improvement, consisting of three company and three union representatives, was mandated to set up a system-wide "quality of work life" program (the committee hired consultant Michael Maccoby to help them organize this "QWL" effort). The two sides also established joint Technology Change Committees—one each in the twenty-three Bell operating companies and two major AT&T divisions—in which the unions could "discuss major technological changes with management before they are introduced" (as part of this provision, the corporation also agreed to provide the unions with six months advance notice of all proposed technological changes). Finally, a national Occupational Job Evaluation Committee was also set up to develop recommendations for the reclassification of jobs in the fast-changing Bell System workplace.

Of the three joint committees, it was the quality of work life program that was the top priority for both management and the unions. According to a recent report sponsored by the U.S. Department of Labor, the Bell System quality of work life program is "one of the largest worker participation programs in the country." And it is certainly among the most comprehensive of such programs in American industry today. At the time of the Bell System divestiture in January 1984, there were more than twelve hundred shop-floor QWL committees in operation throughout AT&T, involving nearly fifteen thousand unionized employees. Both the structure and the goals of the program suggests its "joint" character. All steering committees at both the national and local level are made up of equal numbers of managers and union officials. Training for shop-floor participants was developed jointly by the company and the unions and is carried out by teams of management and union "resource people." The goals of the shop-floor committees also suggest the program's joint approach: both to make work "more satisfying" and to improve "organizational performance and service quality."

The typical shop-floor QWL committee has anywhere from five to nine participants, chosen at random from the volunteers in a particular office or department. Most are unionized employees, including one union shop steward. A first-level management supervisor from the office also participates in committee deliberations. The chairperson is either elected by the group or selected according to criteria that members decide upon among themselves; usually, the role of chairperson rotates throughout the group over time. Each QWL group meets on the average of four hours each month to research shop-floor problems and formulate formal recommendations to upper management. The only restriction on the topics that groups can consider is that they must not involve issues that are part of the formal contractual relationship between company and union—such as wages or work assignments. Recommendations are presented to second-level managers who must respond in writing to the group within two weeks. If a manager should choose to reject a particular committee recommendation, he or she must explain why and suggest possible changes that would make the proposal acceptable.

Unionists who are involved in the Bell System QWL program see it as a way to extend the collective voice of unionism to new issues and new areas of working life. According to former CWA president Glenn Watts, "through QWL, we are extending our influence into the murky territory of 'management prerogatives,' helping to shape management practices and policies while they are being formed rather than after the fact." The idea is that by supplementing the traditional "adversarial" relationship of the collective-bargaining table and formal grievance procedure with a cooperative "problem-solving" relationship between labor and management, the quality of work life program provides unions with a means to address problems that were previously difficult to handle.

Consider the issue of "job pressures," which was probably the primary reason that the telecommunications unions were willing to participate in an industry-wide QWL process. Problems of occupational stress are intimately related to the design of technology, the organization of work, patterns of supervision, and attitudes of office supervisors. But such issues are rarely a part of the formal collective bargaining process. Unionists hope that the quality of work life committees will provide a more flexible structure to address such issues, a means for workers to exercise control over these and other noncontractual matters where it affects them most—in the workplace itself.

While the contract language establishing the QWL progam does not deal directly with new workplace technology, from the very beginning, unionists have also seen the shop-floor QWL committees as an important mechanism to address this particular area of management prerogative. According to the National Bargaining Report sent to all CWA members to explain the 1980 contract, the QWL committees would give workers "an opportunity to participate in the design and implementation of their own jobs."

"Technology presents a major area for the QWL committees to get into," says Yvette Herrera, a CWA staff member and "QWL facilitator" in the union's Chicago area office. "I see the committees getting involved in the design of new technology and facilitating the process of technological change. I think that eventually both of these areas—technology and QWL—will become one."

And for Joe Payne, the Chester, Pennsylvania, telecommunications technician, who has experienced firsthand some of the frustrations of the brave new workplace, QWL holds the potential for restoring to industry technicians some of the traditional autonomy— and respect—of their craft. "I believe that the company needs us more than they need a lot of these first-level managers," says Payne, who has become the chairperson of his local's quality of work life committee. "That's finally what QWL is all about. They're trying to address the needs of the technician, to make him more involved through participatory management. They're trying to raise the craft back to the importance it once had."

In the four years since the telecommunications industry quality of work life program was established, it has made an important difference in day-to-day workplace relations at many AT&T and Bell operating company offices. QWL committees have made recommendations improving the physical office environment. They have helped eliminate some of the more extreme authoritarian practices of AT&T management—through the efforts of a number of QWL groups, for example, telephone operators in many offices no longer have to ask permission to go to the bathroom. According to the 1984 Department of Labor report, quality of work life team members reported levels of job satisfaction 12 percent higher than those in the Bell System as a whole.

In a few cases, the shop-floor committees have gone even further to touch upon issues related to work organization and job design. Some groups, for example, have instituted flextime programs or reorganized office scheduling procedures in order to give workers some choice over their work hours. And in what is perhaps the most dramatic QWL success story, the new Hotel Office Business Information System (HOBIS) office in Tempe, Arizona, was planned in close cooperation with a QWL team. The committee developed a work organization made up of "autonomous work groups" which allowed some 130 office workers to schedule and perform their own jobs without any first-line supervision. The savings resulting from the group's office organization plan (estimated at $200,000 per year in supervisors' salaries alone) have been put aside in a discretionary fund controlled by the committee; it has been used to fund workers' participation in company job training programs.

However, the closer that most committees have come to issues involving the control of new technology—issues that go beyond the immediate workplace to involve company-wide policies and impinge upon the basic prerogatives of AT&T management—the less successful they have been. So much so that the Department of Labor study describes a number of cases where committees began with great excitement and enthusiasm only to reach a point where, in the words of one researcher, they start "running out of gas."

A good example concerns what is perhaps the most deleterious use of computer technology to control human work—computerized productivity monitoring. Workers at AT&T and the Bell operating companies are subject to a daunting range of productivity "indexes" measuring work performance, such as the Average Work Time (AWT) record kept on all operators which compares the number of calls they handle to those of their co-workers. Such measurement systems are one of the greatest sources of job stress in the telecommunications industry.

Some QWL committees (particularly at Bell operator offices) have tried to address the monitoring issue. But according to one unionist involved in the QWL effort, the result has been only "minor tinkering" with industry productivity indexes. In one office, where workers' AWT ratings were made public for everyone to see, the committee convinced the local supervisor to keep them in her office instead; but workers are still rated on their performance according to the AWT measure. In another, the QWL group recommended a six-month grace period for new operators, so that they would not have to worry about their performance while learning the ropes of their new job. But after that period, they were subject to the same measures as everyone else. At the HOBIS office in Arizona, the committee worked out a plan in which everyone's official AWT rating is, in fact, the overall office average. But while all such initiatives succeed in softening the impact of computerized monitoring, none of them actually challenges the idea of monitoring itself or provides workers with influence over how management decides to use it. For example, in April 1984, AT&T Communications suspended and fired an eighteen-year veteran operator named Maevon Garrett because of an "unsatisfactory" AWT (her average time was 87.3 percent as fast as that of her co-workers; in other words, she was taking thirty-three seconds to complete each call rather than thirty). Only after vociferous union protests (including a demonstration at an AT&T stockholders meeting) was Garrett reinstated.

What is true for monitoring and productivity indexes in particular is also true for technology-related issues in general. When it comes to the issues of technology and control, the QWL committees have encountered a major barrier. According to Robert Leventhal, the union staff member responsible for quality of work life programs at the Telecommunications International Union, most committees have yet to move beyond what he calls "environmental issues."

"They get the lounge fixed up, or they get a microwave put into the break room," Leventhal explains. "They do that kind of thing rather than getting into issues about the work process or job redesign." An important reason is that technology and work reorganization ultimately has to do with basic questions about power in the corporation, questions that are beyond the capacity of local committees to address.

"I think there is a sense of hopelessness, a conviction on the part of the groups that there is nothing to be done about the machine," continues Leventhal. "Now, of course, there is. But in order to do something about technology, you'd have to go back all the way to engineering. Somehow, you'd have to involve workers in the stage of design. And that is far beyond the power of either office workers or their local managers."

And according to a 1984 report of the CWA Research Department, "Though the QWL process has led to improved relations and less burdensome supervision in many offices, it has not reached to the fundamental policies which shape the development of new technologies. It seems that for every improvement in individual locations, a dozen systems come from Bell Laboratories reinforcing the dehumanizing patterns which we are battling."

Theoretically, the Technology Change Committees, also established by the 1980 contract, are supposed to be the forum where these broader issues about technology and work can be addressed. Unlike the shop-floor QWL committees, they exist at a much higher level of authority. Each AT&T division and Bell operating company has its own committee, usually consisting of three upper-level corporate managers and three full-time district union officials. What's more, the committees are mandated to deal specifically with issues related to technological change. However, of the three kinds of joint committees established in 1980, the Technology Change Committees have been by far the least successful. Says the TIU's Robert Leventhal: "Basically the whole thing has been a failure."

The contract language setting up the committees describes their purpose as to "attempt to diminish or abolish the detrimental effects of any technological change." And yet, the provision defines no new rights for unions to actually participate in, let alone influence, the corporate decisions crucial to the technology development process. True, the Technology Change Committees, along with the provision for six months advance notice, does give the unions access to certain management information. But the committees are limited to an advisory role. According to the contract, "the Company will advise the union of its plans with respect to the introduction of [technological] changes and will familiarize the union with the progress being made." Then the committees will develop "facts and recommendations so that the company can make well-informed decisions regarding technological change."

AT&T and Bell operating company management have consistently defined the scope of the Technology Change Committees as narrowly as possible, to emphasize their role as a mere "notification" mechanism to help unions and their members better "adapt" to the changes that management has planned for them. Unionists, however, have a substantially broader conception of the committees' role—as a kind of first step toward a major union influence in decisions about how technology is used at work.

According to the CWA's 1980 Settlement Guide, the purpose of the committees is "to alleviate the detrimental effects of changing technology on the work force." The union's 1982 Executive Board Report argues that through the committees, "the union will have a more active role in the way in which new systems are introduced." And in testimony before the House Sub-Committee on Science, Research, and Technology in September 1981, the director of the CWA's Development and Research Department, Ronnie Straw, described the union's ultimate goal as "complete and effective Union involvement in all aspects of technological change, including veto power over the introduction of new equipment."

Thus, from the outset, the cooperative joint Technology Change Committees were divided by a rather substantial conflict of perspectives and interests—with management determined to limit the committees to the narrowest of notification tasks and the union, in its public rhetoric at least, calling for their expansion to include substantial union influence over the process of technology development itself. The result has been an impasse in which, almost without exception, the committees have reflected management's conception and goals.

A Harvard Business School study, conducted in 1983, found that in the first three years of the Technology Change Committee program, more than half of the committees had yet to have a single meeting. Where they had, the management participants had set the agenda, decided what issues would and would not be discussed, and determined just how much information about company plans would be provided to their union counterparts. In some Bell companies, managers went so far as to prepare their formal presentations beforehand with company lawyers, in order to avoid providing union officials with information that might prove useful in collective bargaining (hardly an example of cooperative labor relations dedicated to "problem-solving"). And, in a survey of Technology Change Committee participants, over half of the union representatives who responded reported that management regularly failed to provide them with the mandatory six months advance notice of major technological changes—a clear violation of the 1980 contract. As for the idea of unionists actually influencing company planning and development of new technology, a full 75 percent of union participants said that discussions in their committee had *never* resulted in changes in the implementation of new technical systems or in their design.

As a result, the union officials involved in the Technology Change Committees have the same sense of fatalism about their capacity to shape technology according to the interests of their members that Robert Leventhal describes for workers on the shop floor. "A lot of things happen that we can't exert a great deal of influence over," one CWA committee member told the Harvard researchers. "Even if we could, I don't know what we can do about increasing job pressures, boring jobs, and the like. How do you build satisfaction and interest into these totally automated jobs? We regret that this is happening but we just don't know what to do about it."

According to the 1984 report of the CWA Research Department, the effectiveness of the committees "has been limited by the resistance of management . . . and by the lack of experience of union participants. As a result, membership attitude surveys over the past three years have shown, if anything, increasing levels of discontent with job pressures."

And Robert Staffin, a union official at Joe Payne's local in Pennsylvania and a sometime participant in Technology Change Committee deliberations, was even more blunt: "You go in there and they lay this shit on you. They say, 'Listen, from now on, we're going to do away with all these jobs and centralize this and that.' You sit there and you say, 'Uh-huh.' There is no recourse. All it is is a way of knowing early so you're not quite so surprised. It used to be, you were all of a sudden surprised by the changes. Now, you have six months to get surprised."

Why have the Technology Change Committees been so thoroughly unsuccessful in providing workers and their unions with a meaningful "collective voice" in the technology development process? One reason is the continuing unwillingness of corporate management to relinquish its control over this fundamental area of working life. AT&T and Bell managers seem interested in union participation only to the degree that it does not disrupt managerial power. And management involvement in the committees seems expressly designed to insulate the corporate control of technology from any effective challenge on the part of the telecommunications unions. For example, the typical management representatives on the committees are labor relations personnel; their background is in dealing with unions, not managing technology. The engineers, systems designers, and other technology managers who are responsible for determining how technology will be used in the workplace are rarely committee members. And those labor relations managers who are members often don't even have access to basic information about new technical systems and their expected impacts—putting them in a position of ignorance not all that different from that of their union counterparts. (The one thing on which both management and union respondents to the Harvard Business School survey agree is that the prime obstacle to the effectiveness of the Technology Change Committees is their "lack of timely knowledge about the types of systems to be developed.")

If management has in general been unwilling to let new technology become an issue for genuine negotiation, the telecommunications unions have so far been reluctant to challenge them on it. While unionists in the industry have come to recognize that new technology is a major *problem,* they have yet to devote the resources necessary for developing a comprehensive union strategy for addressing it. Pressed by rank-and-file concerns about job pressures and technological change, they have negotiated highly visible programs like the Technology Change Committees, but they have not followed through by making technology a major union priority.

For the district union officials and staff members who have

served on the committees, it is just one of many other union responsibilities. Many of them are not familiar with the state-of-the-art systems and their impacts on the workforce. And none of the telecommunications unions has insisted that AT&T and Bell management provide the six months advance notice of major technological changes mandated by the 1980 contract. Despite many union statements about gaining influence over the design and implementation of new technical systems, the telecommunications unions have not even come close to mounting the kind of sustained struggle that will, most likely, be necessary in order to win such a role.

This leads to a more general consideration that goes to the heart of the experience in telecommunications during the past four years. Part of the problem facing the unions may well be that technology, as a labor issue, is particularly ill suited for resolution by means of labor-management cooperation. More than any other workplace issue, technology challenges traditional ideas about authority at work. It is the realm where labor and management's conflict of interest is most acute. Because the managerial control of technology is the cornerstone of corporate power in the brave new workplace, it is the last place where unions are likely to benefit from a "joint" approach. "Technology is an incredibly charged issue for managers," says a CWA unionist closely involved in the telecommunications industry quality of work life process. "And that is probably fatal for the cooperative approach."

To the degree that unions define their technology policy primarily in terms of joint actions with management on mutually agreed-upon principles, they run the risk of being held hostage to management's narrow conception of this cooperation—simply because it constitutes the "lowest common denominator," the only activity on which both sides can agree. Or, even worse, unions may find themselves caught in a strategic bind: committed to narrow cooperative programs on the one hand, while corporations continue to use technology to extend their control over work on the other.

In their 1983 contract negotiations, the last involving the Bell System as a unified whole, the Communications Workers union won a few more provisions protecting their members from management's plans for new technology—including a $37 million company-funded training program for workers displaced by technological change. As with similar provisions, this was hailed by both company and union as the fruit of their cooperative relationship and a sign of the CWA's future-oriented unionism. And yet, much like the Technology Change Committees, the program has yet to play a major role in either company or union activity concerning the social implications of technology. Six months after the contract was signed, the training program still did not exist.

Meanwhile, the divestiture of the Bell System has presented the telecommunications unions with yet more threats to their traditional strength in the industry. While the Bell operating companies are engaged in a variety of cooperative programs with the unions, their holding companies are setting up new nonunion subsidiaries to compete in high-technology communications and computer markets, in an attempt to close the unions out of this new growing sector. Confronted with a threat by AT&T to subcontract the work of its service representatives to outside companies, the CWA was forced to agree to the creation of a dual wage system in which new workers assigned to the service representative position will be paid below standard union rates. And, throughout 1984, AT&T laid off some 32,000 employees, the vast majority union workers, without consulting the union leadership in advance. After one layoff of 11,000, the CWA's then-president Glenn Watts reported that he was "shocked."

"We had been told . . . that the company was looking at ways to trim costs," he said, "but we had fully expected that they would consult us." Instead, Watts continued, the announcement "was dropped virtually out of the blue."

No one knows for sure what the outcomes of these trends will be—whether American unionism indeed faces "disastrous decline" or whether it will eventually find a way to effectively address the problems of the brave new workplace. However, one can speculate that the recent corporate attack on labor and the unions' seeming inability to respond may well have unintended consequences similar to those of the previous erosion of union power in the 1920s which contributed to the Great Depression.

What may appear to make sense, viewed from the narrow perspective of corporate management, can prove to be extremely costly and counterproductive, seen from a broader social point of view. By expanding their own power and control over work, the managers of the brave new workplace have undermined the traditional institutional framework regulating working life without putting anything in its place. And to the degree that union leaders have seen cooperation as the primary strategy to cope with change, the central institution designed to protect people's collective interests in the workplace becomes a hostage to this corporate control of work, with no independent alternatives of its own.

The result is the kind of problems touched upon in this book: the overdependence on technology to increase efficiency, with so little attention to the human and social dimensions of work that new technological systems end up creating more rigid work organizations than before; the enthusiastic efforts to elicit worker participation and motivation, but according to a conception of participation so narrowly instrumental that it recapitulates the same manipulations of Taylorism itself; and, finally, new kinds of corporate abuses of power even in the most advanced and flexible of workplaces, abuses whose economic and social costs we have barely begun to calculate.

These examples constitute a pattern. The very efforts of the corporation to cope with change undermines society's ability to do so. The deterioration of the old institutional framework of working life creates a new instability that could prove dangerous for society and the economy as a whole. The solution today may prove to be much the same as it was fifty years ago: to create a social movement with the vision and the power to make the brave new workplace serve more social ends, much as industrial unionism did for the mass-production economy. And just as the distinctive accomplishment of industrial unionism was the establishment of national contracts and union job control, a central goal for this social movement of the brave new workplace will be the social control of the new technology itself.

CONCLUSION

———

POLITICAL VISIONS

———

ANY PERIOD OF RAPID CHANGE presents society with unexpected opportunities as well as unforeseen problems. The emergence of the brave new workplace is no exception. The very economic and technological forces that are the harbingers of potential disruption for many segments of the American workforce and substantial social costs for American society as a whole could also be made to serve quite other ends. The condition is that we choose to do so (as individuals but also as a society), choose to shape the changes traversing working life and harness them to different social goals. In a sense, this requires reinventing technology and work; seeing them not as the products of some ineluctable technological development, autonomous and pure, but as a sometimes messy act of social construction, built upon a foundation of myriad interests and goals.

Until now, work and technology have reflected, almost exclusively, the interests of one institution—the private corporation and the managers who run it. The corporation's logic of profit, competitiveness, and market success at almost any price has defined the ends according to which technology has been designed and used in the workplace. As a result, it has also been the prime determinant of technology's impacts on people. Of course, this is not to say that workers are entirely powerless. On the contrary, they are protesting against this corporate control of work in any way they can. When Dave Boggs informally programs his Strippit 750, when workers at the New York City International Operating Center strike to protest job pressures, when VDT operators engage in acts of "resistance," or when semiconductor production workers like Marta Rojas and Anita Zimmerman take their former employers to court, they are all, one way or another, making their interests known. And this ever-present struggle makes the managerial utopia of a perfectly efficient and eminently humane brave new workplace far more problematic, more fraught with its own contradictions and unintended consequences, than most corporate managers would be willing to admit. At the worst, their desire to extend their own control over work can contradict not only workers' aspirations for autonomy but the very ends of increased productivity and efficiency that are the ostensible reasons for new technology in the first place.

Thus, both equity and efficiency demand that other interests than those of the corporation be introduced into the brave new workplace. Put another way, the inherently social nature of work and technology requires that all social groups and institutions affected by the changes in working life be included—"represented"— in the decisions and choices made about those changes: the workers who actually use technology in the workplace and the unions that represent them; the designers whose technical expertise and talents are so crucial to the proper functioning of new technical systems, but who have little say about the ends to which the technology they create is put; citizens who must live with technology's impacts, whether on the health of their neighborhoods or the quality of the products and services they purchase; and, finally, government officials who approve the vast amounts of public money supporting technological research and development and, more important, are the ultimate representatives of the public good.

What would it mean to open the brave new workplace to these and other groups? How can they possibly play a meaningful role— given the constraints of international competition, the growing complexity of technology and work organization, and the power of the corporation itself? These last pages suggest a few steps that are necessary for this to happen, along with the particular responsibilities of some specific social groups.

As the primary expression of workers' collective voice and collective interests, unions must take the lead in making the brave new workplace an enterprise of social choice. Organized labor, for all its current problems and organizational weakness, still remains the central institution in American society where new rights of participation and power at work will first be articulated, realized, and put into practice. No durable solution to the problems of the brave new workplace is possible without a vigorous renaissance of trade union activity in American industry.

In order for this to happen, however, unions need to look to their past as well as to the future. More specifically, they need to recapture the idea of unionism as a social movement that offers a competing vision of the future, an authentic alternative to the corporate blueprint for the brave new workplace. Such a vision would begin by unequivocally challenging the principle of "management prerogatives" developed during the era of scientific management. And of all the areas of working life that have traditionally been considered the exclusive responsibility of the corporation, the design and development of new workplace technology may prove to be the most important.

The new technologies of the computer and advanced telecommunications constitute the central nervous system of the brave new workplace. The decisions determining their use in the workplace also intimately affect work organization, corporate investment, products and markets, even industrial efficiency itself. A strong labor movement dedicated to the social control of technology would redefine the brave new workplace in terms of traditional union values of equity, solidarity, and work as a cooperative social activity. And the role of a "trade unionism of the brave new workplace" would be to translate those union goals into concrete organizational principles for technology, work, and social life.

Such an effort would require, first of all, articulating new rights for workers and their unions to participate in the design and use of new technology at work—and to participate not merely as performers of certain vital functions (the "roleware" to match certain hardware and software) but as the representatives of important social interests different from those of corporate management.

Some American unions have already taken steps toward defining these new rights. One example is the New Technology Bill of

Rights developed by the International Association of Machinists (representing some 650,000 workers in the machine-tool, metal-working, aerospace, and airline industries). Conceived as an amendment to U.S. labor law, the document states that workers, "through their trade union and bargaining units," should have an "absolute right" to participate in all phases of management planning and decisions "that lead to the introduction of new technology or the changing of the workplace systems design, work processes, and procedures of doing work, including the shutdown or transfer of work, capital, and equipment."

The bill also defines a model for how technology should and should not be used in working life. One provision stipulates that technology should "improve the condition of work and . . . enhance and expand the opportunities for knowledge, skills, and compensation for workers." Another states that workers displaced by technological change "shall be entitled to training, retraining, and subsequent job placement or reemployment"—as a fundamental right of employment. Finally, the Machinists union proposal forbids the use of technology "to monitor, measure, or otherwise control the work practice and work standards of individual workers" as well as uses which threaten worker safety and health or are "destructive of the work environment."

Of course, new rights that are not recognized are really no rights at all. So a labor movement campaign for the social control of technology would also have to formulate a long-term strategy to win corporate recognition of those rights—much as the infant industrial union movement of the 1930s had to fight to win management recognition for the principle of unionism itself. This is perhaps the most difficult step of all. Unions have been so institutionalized for so long in American society that many labor leaders seem to have lost the capacity for waging long-term labor struggles, so much so that now, when unionism is faced with a major corporate attack, many find it difficult to respond. Should a movement to limit the corporate control of work ever gain substantial support in organized labor and the public at large, it is likely that it would face massive political opposition from the American business community. How might unions respond? Put another way, what will be the equivalent in the brave new workplace to the crucial role of the sitdown strikes to win union recognition in the 1930s?

A recent example, from Australia, dramatically suggests that unions may have a great deal more potential power in the brave new workplace than they might think. Appropriately enough, it concerns the unions of the Australian telecommunications industry. When, in the early 1980s, the management of Australia's public telecommunications agency, TELECOM, announced a plan for the comprehensive computerization of that country's telecommunications network, industry unions did not passively accept management's proposals. Instead, they argued that no new technical systems should be introduced without first obtaining union input and approval. And they criticized the model of work organization on which the management plan for technology was based, claiming that, much as has been the case in the United States, it would lead to the fragmentation and deskilling of the telecommunications technician's job.

But the unions didn't stop there. They took their case to the Australian public as well. They argued that TELECOM's plan, by centralizing service and maintenance functions and underestimating the amount of training necessary for those working the system, would cause telephone service to deteriorate. The unions presented an alternative proposal for the computerization of the system, one based on a decentralized work organization of local, worker-run offices. The unions even engaged in some creative industrial action to emphasize workers' importance in running a highly automated system and to cement their alliance with the public. Instead of going out on strike, the technicians in one office simply switched off the computers that collected information about residential customers' long-distance calls for billing. The telephone system worked as well as ever—and the public received free telephone service for a short period of time.

As a result of their multifaceted campaign, the unions were able to win a great deal more than the usual protective measures (which included a "no layoffs" guarantee far beyond any "job security" provision that American unions have recently won). They gained government support for a unique trial between two competing approaches to organizing technology and work. Two computerized switching exchanges were put into operation, one organized according to management's highly centralized model, the other according to the union alternative. The trial demonstrated that TELECOM management did not have a monopoly on organizational efficiency; the union-designed office was at least as efficient as that of management. TELECOM ultimately agreed to a model of work organization and technology that was a compromise between the original management and union proposals. The unions at the Australian telecommunications authority won the crucial right to negotiate with management over the use of new technology at work.

If unions ever are successful in winning similar rights in this country, there is one final task they will have to take up: the creation of new kinds of institutional expertise necessary to put those new rights into practice where it counts the most, in the workplace itself. In part, this means acquiring the technical competence to be able to analyze new technology as it is developed and evaluate its impacts on work. But even more important is developing programs of rank-and-file education, training, and activism around technology issues that teach people how technology can be made to serve their own interests and goals and allow them to contribute their own perspectives to the design of workplace technical systems.

Ironically, this may be where the recent experiments in labor-management quality of work life programs will prove most important. Their ultimate significance may well be not so much in furthering company-union cooperation but in providing unions with the organizational forms and experience necessary to intervene in corporate decision-making at the shop-floor level. Participation in such programs can lead to the development of new kinds of organizational skills for union members, new internal union networks, and ultimately a taste for control on the part of rank-and-file members. (One of the most detailed surveys of union worker attitudes in quality of work life programs—conducted at MIT's Sloan School of Management—found that while cooperative programs rarely lead to increased worker control over corporate decision-making, they do cause workers to identify the acquisition of such control as an important union goal.)

One can imagine a point, in the not-too-distant future, when, frustrated by the limitations of conventional QWL programs, union activists will attempt to push these shop-floor committees beyond "environmental" concerns to more substantial issues of management prerogatives and policy. As management resists such initiatives, unions may develop more independent agendas for worker participation in and influence over working life.

In the end, today's quality of work life programs may be analogous to the company unions of welfare capitalism in the 1920s. Because they were creations of management, such unions were fundamentally flawed as an independent expression of workers' collective voice. Nevertheless, involvement in these company unions taught workers important lessons about how to organize on a company-wide level, lesssons that were put to good use by the independent industrial union movement of the 1930s, when the Depression made the limitations of the company unions clear to most workers.

There are already some signs that American unions may be adopting a more independent perspective on joint labor-management cooperative programs. In their 1983 contract negotiations, the Communications Workers called for the expansion of the Technology Change Committees to include local workplace committees. The proposal was rejected by management, but in 1984, the union developed its own rank-and-file technology training program designed, according to a draft of the course materials, "to convince [members] that workers have a democratic right to be involved in the decisions about how to use new technology." And in the innovative Workplace Democracy project undertaken by the Machinists union at Eastern Airlines, participation is based upon a well-defined framework of new union rights—including seats on the board of directors, access to detailed financial information about the company, and a role in the design of new work systems. (Among other improvements in work organization and job design inspired by this effort, Dave Boggs has been able to work out an informal arrangement with management which allows him to do most of the prototype programming for the Strippit 750 computer-controlled punch press in the Eastern sheetmetal shop.)

Would a strong labor movement for the social control of technology constitute a return to the "adversarial relationship" in American industrial relations? I prefer to think of it as an extension of labor's collective voice and the principle of negotiation and collective bargaining to a whole new area of working life. At times, such negotiation would surely involve competition and conflict as management and union strive to win workers and the public to their varying models for working life. But not all conflict is destructive; sometimes it can be the catalyst for social creativity, as the case of the Australian telecommunications unions suggests. At other times, this negotiation process would surely involve cooperation, as management and union work together to define mutually acceptable criteria for the design of technology and work. Most of all, negotiating the shape of the brave new workplace would bring new values and new perspectives into working life, instead of excluding everything but the narrow goals of the corporation.

This is a profoundly ambitious social agenda, as daunting in its scope and its difficulty as the idea of industrial unionism must have seemed more than fifty years ago. And organized labor, surely, cannot achieve it all alone. But there are other social groups that may find the idea of exercising social choice in the brave new workplace extremely appealing. And labor must begin to reach out to them, whether through traditional union organizing or by forming new kinds of professional alliances.

According to recent research, one occupational category to be heavily hit by the technological transformations of the brave new workplace is the vast number of unorganized clerical workers in the service sector of the U.S. economy. Most of these workers are women; a great many of them, especially in urban areas, are black or members of other minority groups. Perhaps more than any other single occupational group, they are in special need of representation in the brave new workplace.

As computerization spreads up the hierarchical ladder of the corporation, those many members of the baby-boom generation who work in the corporate middle strata are also severely affected.

Despite the popular image of the ambitious and successful "Yuppie," more and more of them are seeing their own career hopes crushed in the squeeze between intensified labor-market competition with their generational brothers and sisters and the diminishing number of places in the upper reaches of the newly rationalized corporation. They constitute a second category of workers with a special interest in the social control of technology and work.

And, finally, more and more high-technology production workers in the semiconductor and computer industries face not only low wages but work environments that threaten their very health. As these new growth industries consolidate and mature (diminishing the possibilities for advancement made possible by rapid economic growth) and as information about the health effects of work with toxic hazards in high-tech industry spreads, they may begin to see through some of the contradictions of the enchanted corporation and start searching for an alternative that a unionism of the brave new workplace could provide.

Some of the most interesting union organizing efforts taking place today are aimed at these occupational groups. Feminist groups such as the National Association of Working Women have joined with labor unions in an effort to link issues of women's clerical work with those of office automation. The alliance has already borne some fruit. In February 1982, employees at the Syracuse, New York, claims benefit office of the Equitable Life Assurance Society—mostly female VDT operators—voted to join District 925 of the Service Employees International Union in an effort to cope with problems caused in part by managerial practices concerning new technology. In November 1984, after a nearly three-year struggle which eventually led to a nationwide boycott of Equitable by the AFL-CIO, the National Organization of Women, and other groups, the workers won a labor contract which, among other provisions, included explicit criteria for the design of computer terminals and office furniture, special rest-breaks for workers engaged in continuous VDT use, limits on computerized monitoring, and advanced notice of forthcoming technological changes.

Unions in the auto and telecommunications industries have also begun to appeal to middle-level technicians and professionals caught in the vise of economic restructuring at big corporations such as AT&T, General Motors, and Ford. And networks of pro-union high-tech workers have been established in Silicon Valley and Massachusetts' Route 128 in a first step down the long road toward unionization. All these initiatives are elements for a broad coalition favoring public participation and social choice in working life.

But perhaps the most important occupational category with which labor should seek a dialogue and, if possible, an alliance is the rapidly expanding professional community of technical personnel whose job is to design and implement the new technologies of working life: the computer scientists, system designers, software engineers, and other professionals whom I have called "technology managers." Because they occupy a strategic role in the ongoing development of the brave new workplace, they are crucial to the creation of an alternative social vision for technology and work.

Trained in the traditions of scientific management, these workers have generally seen their role as that of impartial experts of the workplace whose only task is to construct the most economically efficent and technologically proficient systems possible. Usually, they see the social dimension of working life as either an irrelevancy to be ignored or an obstacle to be eliminated (in the words of one, "replacing a part of the human with a machine"). And even those technology managers who are open to the new idea of "user participation" tend to define that participation as narrowly and instrumentally as possible. As a result, these technical experts have greatly contributed to the erosion of workers' control in the brave new workplace. Despite their veneer of technical impartiality, they have been agents of the corporate control of work.

But what if the entire process of technology design and development was understood differently—not as a matter of impersonal technical calculation, but as a kind of social dialogue among the various interest groups of the corporation? According to this perspective, user participation would extend far beyond the usual functional definition to include the idea of the "user" as a bearer of unique interests and goals. And the process of technology development itself would be defined as a complex "negotiation" in which different social groups bargain with each other over the purposes and functions of new technology and work systems.

If systems design was conceived in this way—as a "social process"—the role of the designer as an impartial technical expert would become obsolete. Instead, he would have to be an arbiter whose professional role and responsibility is to make explicit to different interest groups involved in the design process the various social implications of diverse technical options. The systems designer would help each group determine what uses of technology were acceptable and unacceptable to them. He would strive to reconcile the competing needs and scenarios of corporate management, unions, professional associations, and the like. A "successful" design would be one that met at least some of the interests of all the groups involved in the design process. And the very design of new technology itself would reflect the social dialogue among the various interest groups of the work organization.

One place where some of these ideas are already being put into effect is in Scandinavia. Since the late 1960s, Scandinavian unions and a small but influential group of computer scientists, engineers, and other technical specialists have been engaged in a creative social dialogue about technology and work. The technologists have served as "union consultants" to locals at metalworking shops, chemical refineries, railroad repair centers, insurance offices, and newspapers. They have helped unions explore the impacts of computerized work systems and develop their own independent strategies for influencing them. In the 1970s, these "action research" projects helped articulate new union rights of participation in corporate decisions about the design and use of new workplace technology, rights that have been institutionalized in both formal collective bargaining agreements and "work environment" legislation such as Norway's 1977 Work Environment Act. And as contact with shop-floor workers has led technical specialists to reflect on the assumptions and implications of their own work, they have begun to formulate alternative methods of "systems design" so that unions' social priorities and goals can be reflected in the technology development process. While such initiatives haven't resolved all the problems of the brave new workplace, they have certainly made it easier for workers and the public to make choices about technology design and work organization.

At first glance, it would seem unlikely that American "technology managers" would be interested in a more social conception of their own work. After all, it would challenge their dominant position in the brave new workplace and seem to require them to give up some of their own independence and control. And yet, there are a number of reasons why at least some of these new professionals might be willing to rethink their place in the brave new workplace—reasons that have to do with their emerging and still undefined sense of themselves as members of a distinct profession.

Some will surely be interested in the idea of systems design as a social process out of the simple conviction that the effective design and implementation of new workplace technology depends upon it. They will be willing to extend the idea of user participation beyond the common superficial understanding. Others will embrace this new model of the designer's role out of a growing frustration with their own increasingly constrained possibilities in working life. As computer programming and systems design itself become subject to the same tendencies of rationalization as other occupations, at least some computer technicians and professionals are realizing that the control they thought they enjoyed in the workplace is an illusion. They may welcome the opportunity to play new roles and put their considerable talents in the service of different social goals.

And, of course, it will not require that *all* technology managers take up these ideas for them to have a substantial social impact. Were even a small minority of concerned computer professionals to begin to speak out on the "social responsibility of the systems designer" and, as in Scandinavia, even join together informally and formally with unions and other "user representative" groups in order to create alternative approaches to planning technology and work, then the project to enlarge people's realm of choice in the brave new workplace would take a giant step.

But the problems of the brave new workplace exceed the capacity of particular professional groups or labor unions to address them. They extend to society as a whole. There is no better illustration of this fact than that most elementary dimension of working life, employment itself. The unemployed worker may disappear from the company balance sheet or the union membership roles, but he or she remains a citizen. And while the corporation may be able to "externalize" the costs of economic and technological transformation, society cannot. For this reason, the brave new workplace is also a responsibility of the federal government.

Such an assertion runs against the current of prevailing political wisdom in America—the conservative denial that government has *any* role to play in working life. The Reagan administration has radically diminished the government's presence in the workplace, by dismantling basic worker occupational health and safety protections and by severely limiting union rights. However, behind the political right's ideological attack on the principle of government intervention and regulation, there is a hidden agenda of aggressive government advocacy for business interests in both the workplace and society. This advocacy intimately shapes the major influence the U.S. government *already* enjoys in the brave new workplace—an influence that is as shortsighted as it is profoundly undemocratic.

The major public source of financial support for research and development of new workplace technology, today, is the U.S. Department of Defense. In the past decade, it has spent billions of dollars to make sure that the brave new workplace conforms to the dual imperatives of expanded corporate control and the increasing militarization of economic life. A typical example is the Air Force's Integrated Computer-Aided Manufacturing Project (ICAM). From 1979 to 1984, ICAM spent $100 million in order to make the much-publicized and long-awaited "factory of the future" a reality, by developing the next generation of integrated computerized manufacturing systems. Part of the Air Force's Partners in Preparedness program, ICAM was a generous source of financial largess for some of America's biggest corporations (primarily in the aerospace industry) and most prestigious engineering schools. It provided them with the resources to develop technologies too expensive for any of them to develop on their own. However, there is one social partner that the Air Force left out—the labor unions representing aerospace workers at many of the participating companies. From the beginning, organized labor was excluded from the ICAM Project, and the Air Force repeatedly rejected the requests of the Machinists union for a role in the automation program.

Not surprisingly, many of the recommendations coming out of the ICAM Project reflect the most rigid conception of industrial automation imaginable and the worst assumptions of the perspective that sees technology as an instrument of managerial control. For example, one conclusion is that skill requirements for shop-floor workers in the aerospace industry should be substantially diminished and that state-funded vocational education programs should be downgraded. Given the long and sorry history of corporate attempts to do away with the human element in work, these and other recommendations are extremely dubious. Nevertheless, the damage has already been done.

Even as the government is supporting the most socially narrow conception of the brave new workplace through military-funded projects like ICAM, the Reagan administration has been making it *more* difficult for ordinary citizens to cope with the changes of working life. At a time when the U.S. labor market is on the edge of enormous transformations, Reagan budget cuts at the Department of Labor's Bureau of Labor Statistics have forced government statisticians to limit data collection for the bureau's "occupational outlook" forecasts. As a result, the federal government is less able to provide citizens with useful information about trends in the labor market than it was five years ago.

Government could be made to play a very different role in the brave new workplace. Instead of using taxpayers' dollars to reinforce the corporate control of work, it could target them at initiatives to empower ordinary citizens in their workplaces, unions, and professional associations—help them to develop the resources and skills necessary to effectively exercise influence and choice in working life. This could take place in any number of ways; many of them need not cost a great deal of money nor require the creation of new federal bureaucracies.

To give one simple example, the federal government is probably the largest purchaser of new workplace technology in America today—equipment to be used in its own offices and departments. Were the government to establish a set of social criteria for the design of the computer technology it purchased—ergonomic standards for office automation systems, for example, or procedures mandating federal office worker participation in the development and implementation of new workplace technical systems—the producers of office technology would have to respond. This would have the added impact of shaping the entire technology market. The norms established by the federal government for its own technology would become generalized throughout American industry. Using its own technology-purchasing policy is one relatively straightforward way for the government to support the introduction of social criteria into the brave new workplace.

But the federal government could also do a great deal more. Imagine that a mere tenth of the tax dollars spent on the ICAM Project—$10 million— was devoted to a public program on the social implications of workplace technology. This money would be used to provide funding and expertise to a broad cross section of social and professional groups for the express purpose of helping them expand their participation in the brave new workplace. The government would work with state universities and technological institutes to establish programs for training workers and managers in the social implications of new technology and how to address them. It would support independent union efforts to develop "technology education and training" programs for rank-and-file members and fund experimental projects at nonprofit agencies, public-sector organizations, or worker cooperatives to use new technology to meet social needs. The government might also fund efforts at engineering schools or in computer science departments to develop curricula on "the social responsibility of the computer professional" or "systems design as a social process." It might even sponsor pilot projects in "participatory systems design" at selected workplaces in industry.

Ultimately, the most important role for the federal government may be to sponsor new social legislation designed to institutionalize more effective mechanisms for social intervention in working life. Specific measures might include a nationwide "labor market information system" which would provide the public with accurate and timely information about trends in the labor market; publicly funded and controlled worker retraining programs to encourage the development of new workforce skills; revised U.S. labor law defining new union rights of participation in corporate decision-making; and perhaps even a comprehensive "work environment" act articulating specific society-wide goals and criteria for working life.

Of course, governmental initiatives to open the brave new workplace to the ideas and interests of diverse social groups will require broad public support. And such support can only follow on the widespread conviction among ordinary people that working life can indeed be different and that they have the power to make it so. For this reason, the social control of technology is, finally, a political project, one that replaces the empty illusion of the all-powerful and benevolent corporation with an alternative vision of work as a realm of democratic social choice. Only then will the contradictions of control in the American corporation find their resolution and the brave new workplace begin to reflect the aspirations of all Americans.

INDEX

"active" jobs, 80
Adler, Paul, 105*n.*
Advanced Micro Devices (AMD), 152, 155–60, 161, 164, 167
aerospace industry, 210–11
AFL-CIO, 206
air pollution, Silicon Valley, 163–64
Alienation and Freedom (Blauner), 72
allergies, 139, 145–46, 149
American Economic Association, 176
American Electronics Association, 140
American Federation of Information Processing Societies, 100
Andersen (Arthur B.) & Co., 18, 32
antiunionism, 11, 173–74, 176, 181, 196, 210
Apple Computer, 4
assembly line, 8, 24–25, 78, 135, 176–77; robots on, 16, 21; stresses of, 72–73, 80
AT&T, 16, 44–52, 63–64, 78, 81–82, 185–96, 207; divestiture of, 82, 185, 196; International Operating Center (New York City), 85–89; Work Relationships Survey, 84, 185. *See also* Bell System
Atlantic magazine, 4
Audio Response System (Bell), 20
Australia, 202–203

authoritarianism in workplace, 8–9, 85, 93, 116, 120, 123, 128–30, 177, 188
auto industry, 183–84, 206–207
automating a fiction, 103–105, 107
automation: computerized, 20–28; of manufacturing, 15, 28–30, 36–44, 210–11; origin of term, 25; systems design problems, 103–105, 109; user resistance to, 100–102, 107. *See also* office automation
Averett, Derek, 49–50, 65

Baca, Paula, 155–57, 160, 171
banking industry, 30–31, 109–17; computerization, 105–107, 111–16
Barnett, George, 176
batch manufacturing, 25
Bauerle, Cathy, 147–51
Becker, Ernest, 124
Bell, Daniel, 7–8, 98
Bell Labs, 20, 44–45, 50, 54, 64, 107
Bell of Pennsylvania, 84
Bell System, 44–64; Automated Repair Service Bureau, 61–62; EES, 50–52; ESS, 44–45, 50, 52–55; Electronics Systems Mini-Course, 50–51; job pressures at, 81–89, 185, 187, 189, 193; MLT, 47–50, 82, 105; 1980 union contract, 185–86, 188, 192, 193, 195; productivity index (AWT), 63, 82,